Successful Aging and Well-Being Workbook

Facilitator Reproducible Sessions
for Motivated Behavior Modification

John J. Liptak, EdD
Ester R.A. Leutenberg

wholeperson
Health & Wellness Publishers
Duluth, Minnesota

Health & Wellness Publishers

101 West 2nd Street, Suite 203
Duluth, MN 55802

800-247-6789

books@WholePerson.com
WholePerson.com

Successful Aging and Well-Being Workbook
Facilitator Reproducible Sessions
for Motivated Behavior Modification

Copyright ©2016 by John J. Liptak and Ester R. A. Leutenberg. All rights reserved. Except for short excerpts for review purposes and materials in the activities and handouts sections, no part of this workbook may be reproduced or transmitted in any form by any means, electronic or mechanical without permission in writing from the publisher. Activities and handouts are meant to be photocopied.

All efforts have been made to ensure accuracy of the information contained in this workbook as of the date published. The author(s) and the publisher expressly disclaim responsibility for any adverse effects arising from the use or application of the information contained herein.

Printed in the United States of America
10 9 8 7 6 5 4 3 2 1

Editorial Director: Carlene Sippola
Art Director: Mathew Pawlak

Library of Congress Control Number: 2015917439
ISBN: 978-157025-339-3

Introduction to *Successful Aging and Well-Being Workbook* For the Facilitator

SOME TRUTHS ABOUT AGING:

- People age from the moment they are conceived.
- Growing older in the 21st century is not what it used to be.
- Retirement is changing.
- Old used to mean frail.
- Years ago, over 65 was considered old. People stopped working. Some stopped living a fruitful life.
- The process of aging can be challenging!
- Older people may suffer losses of family members, friends, co-workers, neighbors, etc.
- Older people may experience varying degrees of limitations.
  Mobility
  Independence
  Health, physical and mental

The *Successful Aging and Well-Being Workbook* is designed to help your clients enhance their existing successful aging behaviors and develop new attitudes about aging that will improve the quality of their lives as they age. By completing the assessments, activities, and exercises in this workbook, you will help your clients to achieve the following:

- Experience a better quality of life
- Manage emotions
- Increase self-esteem
- Envision hope for the future
- Live a healthier lifestyle mentally, physically and socially
- Develop and maintain friendships and a social network
- Improve everyday functions
- Live a healthier and more independent life
- Engage in productive activities
- Experience meaning and purpose later in life
- Show resilience when stressed
- Keep a sense of humor

Many people focus on the negative aspects of aging rather than the positive aspects of living in the present and planning for the future. The purpose of this workbook is to help people explore the positive aspects of life that can make aging a more meaningful and successful experience.

Successful Aging and Well-Being Workbook Sections

Observable actions and mannerisms that people display when reacting to life events are called behaviors. Behavior modification involves identifying ineffective behaviors, intentionally targeting them, setting goals for behavioral change, monitoring progress and determining effective rewards for improved behaviors.

The *Mind-Body Wellness Series* is composed of workbooks designed to help people learn how to discontinue old, destructive health habits and adopt new, healthy lifestyle choices. The model, referred to as Motivated Behavior Modification (MBM), looks at specific learned behaviors and the impact of environmental stimuli on those behaviors. It focuses on helping participants change undesirable and unhealthy lifestyle behaviors by objectively identifying unrealistic behaviors and replacing them with healthier, more effective behaviors.

Section 1 – Quality of Life
This section will help participants explore and understand the current quality of their life. Suggestions will be offered to improve their current life.

Section 2 – Emotional Agility
This section will help participants examine how they are feeling, how satisfied they are, and how hopeful they are about the future. Suggestions will be offered to improve their emotional well-being.

Section 3 – Healthy Lifestyle
This section will help participants gauge how healthy their current lifestyle is. Suggestions will be made for ensuring proper sleep, nutrition, and exercise.

Section 4 – Daily Living
This section will help participants explore how well they are functioning daily. Suggestions will be offered to accentuate ways of functioning more effectively.

Section 5 – Sense of Humor
This section will help participants explore how a sense of humor and laughter can release physical, emotional and mental health benefits for themselves and the people around them.

Section 6 – Social Connections
This section will help participants explore how socially active and effective they are. Suggestions will promote a healthy nurturing network of family and friends that can be called on for support and ways to offer support to them.

Section 7 – Productive Aging
This section helps participants explore their use of time and how productive they feel. Suggestions will be provided to enhance work, volunteer, educational, and fun activities.

Changing Unhealthy Behaviors

Developing healthy social functioning can be difficult, as implied in the adage, "It's hard to teach an old dog new tricks!" Social well-being brings a sense of life satisfaction, joy and contentment through relationships with others. However, developing and maintaining healthy relationships takes work! This work can be challenging for participants, but they can successfully develop the skills necessary to be valued in any type of relationship. This workbook uses a model known as MBM (Motivated Behavior Modification). For participants to be successful, the facilitator can enhance their motivation in several ways.

Components of Each MBM Section

1. SELF-ASSESSMENT
Step 1 is the self-assessment of participants' current level of successful aging and well-being. Encourage participants to take one step at a time. By working on one set of behaviors at a time, the task of changing behaviors will not feel insurmountable. Because successful aging and well-being can be difficult to think about, it is important that participants take small steps and work slowly to change ways their interactions affect their lives. It is helpful to change one aspect of healthy aging at a time, so that one is not overwhelmed or discouraged by trying to do too much at once. Encourage participants to keep it simple! Each section is set up in a step format for the MBM toward the successful aging and well-being of each participant.

2. SUPPORT SYSTEM
Step 2 will guide participants to develop a support system of people who can help them achieve their goals of successful aging and well-being. The handouts will encourage them to define who in their lives can help and support them while they learn to develop their successful aging and well-being abilities. Explain to participants that developing a support system will allow them to have people with whom to express their concerns about aging. Explain that each participant's support system will vary for each type of behavior.

3. JOURNALING
Step 3 includes journaling questions to help participants reflect upon their current feelings of aging. Encourage participants to write everything down in a journal. Through journal writing people are able to connect with their past, present, and hopes for their future. Journaling can be therapeutic as well as a way to begin identifying goals for successful aging and well-being.

4. GOAL-SETTING
Step 4 will remind participants not to give up and to be persistent in their efforts to develop greater success. Explain that this takes time and will not achieve immediate results. The purpose of setting goals is to help each participant take smaller steps leading to the selected ultimate goal. Encourage them to review and revise their plans to develop successful aging and well-being skills that lead to greater satisfaction. By developing MBM goals to work toward and achieve, participants can remain motivated while they gradually learn how to live well later in life.

5. MONITORING MY BEHAVIOR
Step 5 will help participants see the progress they are making in developing successful aging and well-being skills. This will assist them in being accountable, persistent, and motivated to improve the quality of their lives now and in the future. Coach and encourage participants to develop and utilize their newfound successful aging and well-being skills.

6. REWARD YOURSELF
Step 6 will enthuse participants by selecting rewards for themselves as they achieve their successful and well-being goals. Remind participants to reward themselves as they improve. HEALTHY rewards provide them with positive feedback and motivation to continue developing successful and well-being skills.

7. TIPS
Step 7 will assist participants to gain ideas by reading and implementing various tips which are included as suggestions for processing each section.

Motivational Barriers to Behavioral Change

With successful aging and well-being, people will develop the skills necessary to ensure that they make the most out of their years later in life. However, changing behavior is not an easy task, and many barriers exist on the path to successful and well-being behavioral change. Participants must remain motivated for their behaviors to change and realize that one is never too old to learn new skills. When participants begin to see their behavior changing, they will feel more confidence and enthusiasm in approaching new learning situations. Therefore, as the facilitator, you can be aware of any barriers that may be keeping participants from being successful as they work to be positive and productive in aging successfully.

Motivation is one of the keys to success in reaching goals. Motivation is an inner desire to reach a goal through effective action. Following are some of the keys in overcoming motivational barriers:

- Motivation can be accomplished through negative and positive means. Negative motivation is usually accomplished through the use of punishment. This is not the method to use when trying to motivate. Instead, relying on positive motivation or rewards is the way to ensure that successful aging and well-being continues.

- Some people feel very motivated when they begin to learn new skills. How many times have we all set New Year's resolutions? When we do, we feel motivated when beginning, but soon fall back into old habits that are less effective. The answer is to make long-lasting behavioral changes to work on our goals at a steady pace.

- Failure, like success, is a result of taking action. One of the biggest motivational barriers is fear of failure, or fear that the outcome will not result in what we wish.

- We must accept that we will not always be successful in our efforts to make major behavioral changes. We may not make all of the changes desired, but that doesn't mean we stop doing what we're doing. Our hope is that we give our very best and hope for the best.

- Some people may get bored working on changing the same behavior for too long. Boredom can kill motivation. Try working on enjoyable aspects of successful aging and well-being whenever you feel your participants are on the verge of burning out or giving up.

Achieving fulfillment and satisfaction in all aspects of life contributes to successful aging and well-being. In working to enhance successful aging and well-being, participants need to remember that the task may not be easy and will require practical application. Therefore, it is important to understand the variety of aspects related to aging successfully. This workbook is designed to help your participants function effectively emotionally, cognitively, and physically; use their time productively; continue to engage in fulfilling social relationships; and function effectively in everyday life.

Using the *Successful Aging and Well-Being Workbook* to Modify Behavior

Behavior Modification programs provide a process to change destructive ways of aging and replace those negative behaviors with positive behaviors that will lead to greater health and well-being. The behavior modification program included in this series of workbooks contains several critical components.

Motivated Behavior Modification (MBM) Components

STEP 1: Self-Assessment – The first step in modifying behavior involves determining the frequency, circumstances, and outcomes of successful aging and well-being that needs to be altered or enhanced. MBM relies on objective self-assessment to determine the participants' aging functioning to establish baselines of strengths and limitations. Once a baseline is established, the data collected can be used to track participants' progress in the aging functions that are being addressed. The self-assessments contained in this workbook are referred to as "formative assessments" and can be used to assess each participant's current level of functioning and also to measure aging functioning change over time.

In this stage, people acknowledge that they are feeling the effects of getting older and seriously thinking about making healthier lifestyle changes. Self-assessments are powerful tools for helping participants learn more about themselves and to gain valuable insights into their ways of behaving. Self-assessments also allow facilitators to gather information and see a complete picture of each person's thoughts, feeling and behaviors.

Facts about self-assessments

- Self-assessments provide you with a small sample of behavior and should not be used to stereotype participants. They are designed to allow participants to explore their behavioral strengths and weaknesses.
- Factors such as cultural background, handicaps, and age should be taken into consideration when exploring self-assessment results.
- Self-assessments are designed to be self-administered, scored and interpreted by the participants. However, facilitators need to be available to assist participants in understanding their scores in an objective and helpful way.
- Self-assessments are designed to gather self-reported data, thus the results are dependent on each participant's motivation and cooperation.
- Self-assessment results should be explored in light of other behavioral data facilitators have available, not in isolation.
- Self-assessments can be used with individual participants or with groups.
- Self-assessments can be used to form specific decisions about the type of instruction that would be most beneficial. Thus, if members of the group score lowest on a particular self-assessment for a section, that might be an effective place to concentrate instruction.
- Participants can use the results of their self-assessments to adjust and improve their behavior.

(Continued on the next page)

Using the *Successful Aging and Well-Being Workbook* to Modify Behavior

Motivated Behavior Modification (MBM) Components *(Continued)*

STEP 2: Support System – The next step in behavior modification involves participants recognizing who is in their support system and identifying which people are supportive of which topics. This requires participants to think about who can support them through each particular behavior modification, what their supporters can do, and how they will help. Support people may vary for each behavior. The person who is being supportive about cognitive functioning can be different from the one being supportive about exploring the importance of living a healthy lifestyle.

STEP 3: Journaling – The next step in behavior modification is journaling responses to specific questions. Journaling has been shown to be very effective in helping people to think critically about themselves and issues with which they are coping. It is wise to remind participants not to concern themselves with grammar or spelling. Free-writing thoughts and ideas is the purpose of the journaling pages.

STEP 4: Goal Setting – The next step in behavior modification is to set goals to modify behavior. Goals initiate an action plan and are necessary to motivate behavioral change. Participants will set goals that will replace their old, negative habits with new, healthier habits. It is important to help participants determine which specific behaviors they want to change. This will help to give order and context to the change process. Goals provide participants with direction, priorities, and a well-conceived action plan for MBM. Goals should meet these criteria:

- **Specific and Behavioral:** Goals must be stated in concrete, behavioral terms. For example, "I would like to begin studying at the community college," would be a concrete, behavioral goal.
- **Measurable:** Goals must be measurable so that people can track their progress. For example, "I want to learn something," is too vague to be measured accurately, but "I want to study Spanish at the community college starting in the fall semester," can be measured.
- **Attainable:** Goals must be within reach or participants will not be motivated to work toward them. They must feel that they have a realistic opportunity to achieve their goals. For example, "I will apply for admissions to the community college by May," is an attainable goal.
- **Relevant:** Goals must be important to the participant. For example, learning a second language can help keep a person's brain young and aid in communicating with people in the community. This will help to provide motivation.
- **Time-Specific:** Goals must have specific times for completion if they are going to have power. However, the time frames need to be reasonable and realistic so that participants will feel committed. For example, by setting a goal of "I want to apply for admissions to the community college by summer so I can begin taking classes in the fall," sets a realistic time frame to accomplish the goal. The goal setting process helps participants to be personally accountable in changing their unhealthy behaviors.

STEP 5: Monitoring – The next step is to monitor behaviors until desired outcomes are reached. Sections will be included for participants to keep a regular record of their activities and progress. Motivation is the intrinsic drive that pushes participants into action and makes permanent behavioral changes. Motivation is enhanced when participants are working toward specific goals and monitoring their progress as they continue to make motivated behavioral modifications. By monitoring their progress as they move toward goals, participants reinforce MBM.

STEP 6: Rewards – This step defines rewards for accomplishing behavioral goals. Healthy rewards will vary from person to person. Participants will benefit by rewarding themselves for any positive steps taken to change unhealthy behaviors.

STEP 7: Tips – This final step provides insights into ways people can deal with unwanted behaviors.

Successful Aging and Well-Being Workbook
Introduction for the Participant

Due to remarkable advances in medical technology, life expectancies have increased tremendously. Today, society emphasizes maintaining a good quality of life, emotional agility, healthy lifestyle, satisfying daily life, humor, social connections and productivity. Successful aging and well-being can be described as the factors that permit people to continue daily living effectively – mentally, cognitively, emotionally, and socially – as they age.

Developing and maintaining successful aging and well-being attitudes and behaviors will help you in a wide variety of ways:

- You will be as productive as you can be.
- You will be more enjoyable to be with.
- You will build a social network.
- You will develop and maintain friendships.
- You will experience a better quality of life.
- You will experience a sense of purpose in your life.
- You will experience greater physical health.
- You will feel good about yourself.
- You will have a good sense of humor and have fun.
- You will increase your energy level.
- You will live a healthier lifestyle.
- You will live a more independent life.
- You will maintain hope for the future.
- You will remain mentally active.
- You will show resilience when stressed.
- You will wake up in the morning, knowing that you have something to look forward to each day.

As you can see above, you have many reasons to develop successful aging skills and habits. The biggest challenge is to become motivated to make behavioral changes, and then develop a plan and set goals to enhance how well you age.

The purpose of the *Successful Aging and Well-Being Workbook* is to help you understand the relationship between aging effectively and your overall well-being, and to keep you motivated while you develop effective successful aging skills. In this workbook, you will engage in various types of self-assessments. You will have an opportunity to set effective successful aging and well-being goals, and you will continue to look forward to living a healthy life.

(Continued on the next page)

Successful Aging and Well-Being Workbook
Introduction for the Participant *(Continued)*

Some Things to Remember … You can do this!

- **Take one step at a time.** By working on one behavior at a time, the task of changing your behavior will not feel insurmountable. Because changing any habit or behavior takes time, it is important to start with small things and work slowly to change one at a time.

- **Create a support system.** Who can you ask for help and support in modifying your successful aging and well-being behaviors? Choose people with whom you feel comfortable, and people who would understand that you are trying to make some changes in a specific area of your life. You can develop new, more effective aging skills, let people know about your desire to change, and allow them to support you.

- **Write everything down.** Saying you are going to make changes is not enough. The activities in this workbook will help you to do that.

- **Be persistent in your effort and do not to give up on yourself.** Remember that it takes time to change ineffective relationship patterns. Do not expect immediate results. The purpose of setting goals is to help yourself take smaller steps leading to your overall goal. Plan for a healthier lifestyle. By developing motivated behavior modification (MBM) goals to work toward and achieve, you will remain motivated while you gradually turn unhealthy habits into healthy ones.

- **Be accountable.** If during your efforts to make positive changes you slip and go back to previous ways of functioning, don't let this stop you. Learn from your setbacks and use your newfound knowledge to make successful choices. Monitor your progress.

- **Reward yourself.** Healthy rewards provide you with positive feedback and motivate you to continue in your efforts to develop greater skills. You will find ways to reward yourself for a job well done!

- **Consider the tips, as applicable to you,** provided on the last page of each of the sections.

You are now prepared to begin making motivated behavior modifications. Working through the steps in each section of this workbook will allow you to more easily develop healthy, effective ways to age successfully. This process really works. It is an exciting way to change old, ineffective patterns and begin to enjoy and appreciate a happier, healthier life.

Table of Contents

Section I – Quality of Life
Step 1: Self-Assessment Introduction and Directions 17
    Self-Assessment 18
    Self-Assessment Scoring Directions, Profile Interpretations and Descriptions 19
Step 2: Recognize and Develop a Support System 20
Step 3: Quality of Life Journaling 21
Step 4: Set Goals 22
Step 5: Monitor My Mobility Behavior 23
    Monitor My Aspects of Mobility 24
    Monitor My Health Behavior 25
    Monitor My Current Health Behavior 26
    Monitor My Positive Outlook Behavior 27
    Monitor Characteristics of a Positive Outlook 28
Step 6: Reward Myself 29
Step 7: Tips for Motivated Behavior Modifications 30

Section II – Emotional Agility
Step 1: Self-Assessment Introduction and Directions 33
    Self-Assessment 34
    Self-Assessment Scoring Directions, Profile Interpretations and Descriptions 35
Step 2: Recognize and Develop a Support System 36
Step 3: Feelings Journaling 37
Step 4: Set Goals 38
Step 5: Monitor My Emotions Behavior 39
    Monitor My Positive and Negative Emotions Behavior 40
    Monitor My Life Satisfaction Behavior 41
    Monitor My Life Satisfaction Behavior - Quotation 42
    Monitor My Hopeful Behavior 43
    Monitor My Hopeful Aspects Behavior 44
Step 6: Reward Myself 45
Step 7: Tips for Motivated Behavior Modifications 46

Table of Contents

Section III – Healthy Lifestyle
Step 1: Self-Assessment Introduction and Directions 49
      Self-Assessment 50
      Self-Assessment Scoring Directions, Profile Interpretations and Descriptions 51
Step 2: Recognize and Develop a Support System 52
Step 3: Health Journaling 53
Step 4: Set Goals 54
Step 5: Monitor My Sleep Behavior 55
      Monitor My Sleep Behavior - Rating 56
      Monitor My Exercise Behavior 57
      Monitor My Form of Exercise Behavior 58
      Monitor My Nutrition Behavior 59
      Monitor My Nutritional Habits Behavior 60
Step 6: Reward Myself 61
Step 7: Tips for Motivated Behavior Modifications 62

Section IV – Daily Living
Step 1: Self-Assessment Introduction and Directions 65
      Self-Assessment 66
      Self-Assessment Scoring Directions, Profile Interpretations and Descriptions 67
Step 2: Recognize and Develop a Support System 68
Step 3: Daily Living Journaling 69
Step 4: Set Goals 70
Step 5: Monitor My Worry Behavior 71
      Monitor My Spirituality Behavior 72
      Monitor My Medical Behavior 73
      Monitor My Self-Care Behavior 74
      Monitor My Daily Living Behavior 75
Step 6: Reward Myself 76
Step 7: Tips for Motivated Behavior Modifications 77

Section V – Sense of Humor
Step 1: Self-Assessment Introduction and Directions 81
      Self-Assessment 82
      Self-Assessment Scoring Directions, Profile Interpretations and Descriptions 83
Step 2: Recognize and Develop a Support System 84
Step 3: Sense of Humor Journaling 85
Step 4: Set Goals 86
Step 5: Monitor My Humor Behavior 87
      Monitor My Laughter Behavior 88
      Monitor My Sense of Humor Quotation Behavior 89
Step 6: Reward Myself 90
Step 7: Tips for Motivated Behavior Modifications 91

Table of Contents

Section VI – Social Connections
Step 1: Self-Assessment Introduction and Directions.................................95
    Self-Assessment..96
    Self-Assessment Scoring Directions, Profile Interpretations and Descriptions......97
Step 2: Recognize and Develop a Support System.....................................98
Step 3: Daily Living Journaling..99
Step 4: Set Goals..100
Step 5: Monitor My Humanitarian Behavior..101
    Monitor My Humanitarian Relationships Behavior.................................102
    Monitor My Active Life Behavior..103
    Monitor My Activities Behavior..104
    Monitor Developing My Social Network Behavior.................................105
    Monitor My Social Network Behavior..106
Step 6: Reward Myself..107
Step 7: Tips for Motivated Behavior Modifications..................................108

Section VII – Productive Aging
Step 1: Self-Assessment Introduction and Directions...............................111
    Self-Assessment..112
    Self-Assessment Scoring Directions, Profile Interpretations and Descriptions......113
Step 2: Recognize and Develop a Support System...................................114
Step 3: Activities Journaling..115
Step 4: Set Goals..116
Step 5: Monitor My Education Behavior...117
    Monitor My Education Behavior - Opportunities..................................118
    Monitor My Work Behavior...119
    Monitor My Work Behavior - Opportunities...120
    Monitor My Volunteer Behavior...121
    Monitor My Volunteer Behavior - Opportunities..................................122
    Monitor My Fun Behavior..123
    Monitor My Fun Behavior - Activities..124
Step 6: Reward Myself..125
Step 7: Tips for Motivated Behavior Modifications..................................126

Our thanks to these professionals who make us look good!

Cover Art Director	—	Joy Dey
Art Director	—	Mathew Pawlak
Editorial Director	—	Carlene Sippola
Editor and Lifelong Teacher	—	Eileen Regen
Proofreader	—	Jay Leutenberg
Reviewer and Skills Expert	—	Carol Butler

SECTION I

QUALITY OF LIFE

*If standard of living is your number one objective,
quality of life almost never improves.
But if quality of life is your number one objective,
standard of living invariably improves.*

– Zig Zigler

Name_____

Date_____

SUCCESSFUL AGING AND WELL-BEING

QUALITY OF LIFE

Section I: Skills Emphasized in Each Activity Handout

Step 1: Self-Assessment
Respond to a set of prompts, self-score, and interpret personal profile on three scales: mobility, health, and positive outlook.

Step 2: Recognize and Develop a Support System
Identify possible quality of life supporters, types of support they can provide, and their contact information.

Step 3: Quality of Life Journaling
Document activities one is able to do that promote physical and emotional health and a positive outlook. Note each activity's frequency. If increased frequency would be beneficial, identify barriers to performing the activity more often.

Step 4: Set Goals
Set goals that are specific, measureable, attainable, realistic, and time-specific. Identify ways to improve and maintain quality of life. Note how these goals enhance successful aging.

Step 5: Monitor My Mobility Behavior
Identify a behavioral change and goal related to mobility. Document dates, accomplishments, and resultant feelings on a behavioral log.

Monitor My Aspects of Mobility
Describe aspects of mobility, personal challenges, and ways to adapt.

Monitor My Health Behavior
Identify a behavioral change and goal related to health. Document dates, accomplishments, and resultant feelings on a behavioral log.

Monitor My Current Health
Describe ways one is healthy, resultant feelings, and ways to maintain health. Document ways one is unhealthy, resultant feelings, and ways to improve health.

Monitor My Positive Outlook Behavior
Identify a behavioral change and goal related to positive outlook. Document dates, accomplishments, and resultant feelings on a behavioral log.

Monitor Characteristics of a Positive Outlook
Show personal perceptions of a positive outlook through drawings, doodles, and/or words.

Step 6: Reward Myself
Describe four categories of rewards: meaningful, small, can be enjoyed alone, and fun to do with others.

Step 7: Tips for Motivated Behavior Modification
Acknowledge suggestions in these quality of life categories: mobility, health, and positive outlook.

SUCCESSFUL AGING AND WELL-BEING

QUALITY OF LIFE

Step 1: Self-Assessment Introduction and Directions

Quality of life can mean many different things to different people. Quality of life can cover a variety of different areas including standard of living, overall health, relationships, and housing. As people get older, some very important aspects of quality of life include health, mobility, independence, productivity, and a positive outlook about life.

The purpose of the *Quality of Life Self-Assessment* is to help you explore the strength of your current quality of life. Read each statement carefully and circle the number of the response that describes you best.

In the following example, the circled 3 indicates that the statement is very true for the person completing the assessment.

	VERY TRUE	SOMEWHAT TRUE	NOT TRUE
1. I can get around easily	(3)	2	1

This is not a test and there are no right or wrong answers. Do not spend too much time thinking about your answers. Your initial response will be the most true for you. Be sure to respond to every statement.

SUCCESSFUL AGING AND WELL-BEING

QUALITY OF LIFE

Step 1: Self-Assessment

	VERY TRUE	SOMEWHAT TRUE	NOT TRUE
1. I can get around easily	3	2	1
2. I drive a car	3	2	1
3. I am physically active	3	2	1
4. I lift things I need to	3	2	1
5. I move and control my bodily movements	3	2	1
6. I can perform basic self-care activities	3	2	1
7. I have no physical limitations	3	2	1

M. TOTAL = _____

	VERY TRUE	SOMEWHAT TRUE	NOT TRUE
1. I am energetic	3	2	1
2. I am not sick very often	3	2	1
3. I live relatively pain free with or without meds	3	2	1
4. I am able to hear well with or without aides	3	2	1
5. I am able to see well with or without glasses or contacts	3	2	1
6. I engage in activities I enjoy	3	2	1
7. I am understood by others	3	2	1

H. TOTAL = _____

	VERY TRUE	SOMEWHAT TRUE	NOT TRUE
1. I feel that life is meaningful	3	2	1
2. I look forward to the future	3	2	1
3. I am satisfied with how I am living my life	3	2	1
4. I enjoy life and laugh	3	2	1
5. I have many positive experiences	3	2	1
6. I feel a deep inner peace	3	2	1
7. I am grateful for my blessings	3	2	1

P. TOTAL = _____

SUCCESSFUL AGING AND WELL-BEING

QUALITY OF LIFE

Step 1: Self-Assessment Scoring Directions

Quality of life is important for all people. As people age, their quality of life often goes down. The self-assessment you just completed is designed to help you explore the quality of your life.

For each of the items on the previous page, total the scores you circled in each section. Add your circled numbers and put that total on the line marked TOTAL at the end of the section and then transfer that number below.

M. Mobility   Total = _____
H. Health   Total = _____
P. Positive Outlook Total = _____

Profile Interpretation

Find the range for your scores and use the information below to assist you in the interpretation of your scores.

Total Self-Assessment Scores	Result	Indications
Scores from 17 to 21	High	You are experiencing a high quality of life in this area.
Scores from 12 to 16	Moderate	You are experiencing a moderate quality of life in this area.
Scores from 7 to 11	Low	You are experiencing a low quality of life in this area.

Self-Assessment Descriptions

Mobility – People scoring high on this self-assessment are able to get around, have no or limited physical limitations, and can care for themselves.

Health – People scoring high on this self-assessment have energy and enjoy general good health.

Positive Outlook – People scoring high on this self-assessment appreciate their life and believe that it is meaningful, positive and satisfying.

There may be some aspects of life that cannot change, but there are often other ways to adapt, and make up for them.

SUCCESSFUL AGING AND WELL-BEING

QUALITY OF LIFE

Step 2: Recognize and Develop a Support System

Supportive people in your life can help you to further develop your skills. They can help you to live a healthier lifestyle, remain active, maintain social relationships and stay sharp mentally. Complete the following table with people who might be in your support system.

Supporter	How This Person Can Support Me	How I Can Contact This Person
Example: My friend Joanne	She goes to an exercise class and can encourage me to go with her.	Email: Joanne@ooo.com Phone and Text: 000-000-0000
Example: My therapist Greg	He listens, and helps me see things in a way I hadn't before. It helps me if I go more regularly.	Phone: 111-111-1111

Keep this list handy. Call, email or text when you need support.

SUCCESSFUL AGING AND WELL-BEING

QUALITY OF LIFE

Step 3: Quality of Life Journaling

The following journaling questions are designed to help you explore the physical, mental, and social aspects of the quality of your current life.

What physical health activities are you able to do? _____
_____

How often do you do them? _____

Would it be beneficial to do them more often? _____

If your response is yes, what stops you? If your response is no, why not? _____
_____
_____

What mental health-related activities are you able to do? _____
_____
_____

How often do you do them? _____

Would it be beneficial to do them more often? _____

If your response is yes, what stops you? If your response is no, why not? _____
_____
_____

What social activities are you able to do? _____
_____
_____

How often do you do them? _____

Would it be beneficial to do them more often? _____

If your response is yes, what stops you? If your response is no, why not? _____
_____
_____

© 2016 WHOLE PERSON ASSOCIATES, 101 WEST 2ND STREET, SUITE 203, DULUTH MN 55802 • 800-247-6789 • WHOLEPERSON.COM

SUCCESSFUL AGING AND WELL-BEING

QUALITY OF LIFE

Step 4: Set Goals

In order to enjoy a good quality of life, you need to develop goals that will help you increase and maintain your mobility, health and positive outlook skills. These are goals you can work toward, and when completed, will motivate you to do even more! Complete the action plan below, noting the SMART steps required to reach your goals.

Goals need to be SMART:

Specific, **M**easureable, **A**ttainable, **R**ealistic, and **T**ime-Specific

Goals	How I Will Measure This Goal	How This Goal is Attainable and Realistic	Time Deadline	How This Will Help Me
Example: To be more positive	The number of times I look at the glass as half full.	I will journal about each time.	End of this month.	Others will enjoy being around me more.

If you are having trouble identifying goals, consult TIPS, page 30.

SUCCESSFUL AGING AND WELL-BEING

QUALITY OF LIFE

Step 5: Monitor My Mobility Behavior

Monitoring your progress toward developing and maintaining new relationships with co-workers or people in your community is important. Keeping track of your behaviors through logs will help you determine your success in developing new relationships at given times. Periodic re-evaluations support your success. Once you reach your goal(s), set new ones to improve or maintain what you have already achieved. Use a separate page if you need to.

EXAMPLE:

My mobility behavior change *Learn about local transportation options.*
My goal *To shop for myself.*

Date	My Accomplishment	How It Felt
March 31	I can now buy my own groceries.	It felt great!

✂ -

Mobility

My mobility behavior change _____

My goal _____

Date	My Accomplishment	How It Felt

SUCCESSFUL AGING AND WELL-BEING

QUALITY OF LIFE

Step 5: Monitor My Aspects of Mobility

In the spaces that follow, identify the ways you are challenged, and how you can adapt.
(Examples: walk inside or outside; stand; climb stairs; lift or reach; get dressed, bathe, or groom; drive; etc.).

Aspects of Mobility	Ways I am Challenged	How I Can Adapt
Example: Walk outside	I can't walk alone for fear of falling.	Ask a teenage neighbor to walk with me and either pay him or pack his lunches for him.

Share the ways you've adapted and ask others to share with you.

SUCCESSFUL AGING AND WELL-BEING

QUALITY OF LIFE

Step 5: Monitor My Health Behavior

Maintaining good health in your life is critical for your continued successful aging. Keeping track of your behaviors with these people through logs will help you determine what you have accomplished at given times. Periodic re-evaluations support your success. Once you reach your goal(s), set new ones to become even healthier. Use a separate page for each change.

EXAMPLE:

My health behavior change   I will go to a specialist.

My goal   To be able to communicate with others.

Date	My Accomplishment	How It Felt
Feb. 23	I was fitted for a hearing aid.	It feels great to hear better!

✂ ---

Health

My health behavior change _____

My goal _____

Date	My Accomplishment	How It Felt

SUCCESSFUL AGING AND WELL-BEING

QUALITY OF LIFE

Step 5: Monitor My Current Health Behavior

It is important to explore your current healthy (and unhealthy) behaviors.

In the table that follows, identify the ways you are healthy.

Ways I Am Healthy	How It Makes Me Feel	How I Can Continue
Example: I am a healthy weight.	Satisfied when my tests show how my weight change has made a difference.	Exercise and stick to my food plan.

Next, identify the ways you are unhealthy.

Ways I Am Not Healthy	How It Makes Me Feel	How I Can Be Healthier
Example: I have terrible headaches.	Terrible because I am always cancelling my social plans.	Go to the doctor again, and then pay attention to her recommendations.

SUCCESSFUL AGING AND WELL-BEING

QUALITY OF LIFE

Step 5: Monitor My Positive Outlook Behavior

Maintaining a positive outlook in life is important for everyone, especially the older you get! Monitoring your progress toward your goals will help you become even more positive. Keeping track of your behaviors through logs will help you determine what you have accomplished. Periodic re-evaluations support your success. As you achieve your goals, set new ones to improve or maintain what you have already achieved. Use a separate page for each way you want to develop a more positive outlook about your life.

EXAMPLE:

My positive outlook behavior change *To focus on family member's positive qualities.*

My goal *To sincerely compliment family members.*

Date	My Accomplishment	How It Felt
March 31	I told my family how much I appreciate them.	Proud of myself, and of them!

✂ -

Positive Outlook

My positive outlook behavior change _____

My goal _____

Date	My Accomplishment	How It Felt

SUCCESSFUL AGING AND WELL-BEING

QUALITY OF LIFE

Step 5: Monitor Characteristics of a Positive Outlook

In the space that follows, write some words (hopeful, satisfying, spiritual, etc.), or if you prefer draw or doodle, some characteristics that describe what a positive outlook means to you.

List a few aspects of your life in which you need to work on building a more positive outlook.

_____

_____

_____

SUCCESSFUL AGING AND WELL-BEING

QUALITY OF LIFE

Step 6: Reward Myself

Hopefully, you are becoming aware of why it is important to develop and maintain a good quality of life. Congratulations! You need to give yourself a pat on the back or some other reward. People who reward themselves are more likely to continue improving their life! Your reward needs to be something that will give you the incentive to continue to do so. It needs to be healthy, within your budget and something you'll be excited about. If you are buying yourself something, be sure your reward is something you wouldn't ordinarily buy or do.

Brainstorm some of the various ways you could reward yourself. Feel free to write, draw or doodle.

Rewards that Would be Meaningful to Me	Small Rewards I Can Give Myself
Rewards I Can Enjoy Alone	**Rewards that Would be Fun to do with Others**

Pat yourself on the back for the good work you are completing in this section. Rewards help you to pay attention to your triumphs. Rewards will create good feelings and propel you to want to work harder to reach your goals. Whenever you have completed or achieved one of your goals, treat yourself to one of the items you described.

SUCCESSFUL AGING AND WELL-BEING

QUALITY OF LIFE

Step 7: Tips For Motivated Behavior Modifications

Tips for Developing Mobility
- Think about positive adaptations you can make in your living situation to feel safer. (A therapist can help you.)
- Identify obstacles you face and think about ways to overcome these obstacles.
- What would your perfect living situation look like? Identify how you can change your environment to obtain, or come close to, your perfect living situation.
- Explore available methods of transportation that you could use regularly.
- Identify friends and family who can help you to be more mobile.

Tips for Improving Health
- Stop smoking!
- Watch your alcohol intake and limit food with high acidic content.
- Limit factory prepared foods.
- Eat food with high antioxidant content.
- Schedule regular general and specialist, physical and mental health practitioner exams.
- Take your medical practitioner's advice.

If you question it, get a second or third opinion.

Tips for Enhancing Positive Outlook in Life
- Remind yourself that you are special and one-of-a-kind.
- Count ALL of your blessings. These blessings might be related to your family life, your professional life, your social life, where you live, and the world in general.
- Be aware that the future can hold promise and opportunity. Do whatever needs to be done to identify this promise and those opportunities.
- Remind yourself that you can still have dreams you hope to realize.
- Do not put limits on yourself just because of your age.
- Avoid wasting time and energy worrying about what might happen or might not happen in the future – think about what you can do today.

SECTION II

EMOTIONAL AGILITY

*It's so important to realize that every time you get upset,
it drains your emotional energy.
Losing your cool makes you tired.
Getting angry a lot messes with your health.*

– **Joyce Meyer**

Name _____

Date _____

SUCCESSFUL AGING AND WELL-BEING

EMOTIONAL AGILITY

Section I: Skills Emphasized in Each Activity Handout

Step 1: Self-Assessment
Respond to a set of prompts, self-score, and interpret personal profile on three scales: feelings, life satisfaction, and hope.

Step 2: Recognize and Develop a Support System
Identify possible emotional agility supporters, types of support they can provide, and their contact information.

Step 3: Feelings Journaling
Describe what one does and does not feel good about currently. Identify one's greatest satisfaction from the past. Document what to look forward to and concerns about the future. Personalize a quote by identifying which "best and most beautiful things" are felt in one's heart.

Step 4: Set Goals
Set goals that are specific, measureable, attainable, realistic, and time-specific. Identify ways to improve and maintain emotional agility. Note how these goals enhance successful aging.

Step 5: Monitor My Emotions Behavior
Identify a behavioral change and goal related to emotions. Document dates, accomplishments, and resultant feelings on a behavioral log.
Monitor My Positive and Negative Emotions Behavior
Describe one's positive emotions and how to maintain them. Describe one's negative emotions and ways to view situations more positively.
Monitor My Life Satisfaction Behavior
Identify a behavioral change and goal related to life satisfaction. Document dates, accomplishments, and resultant feelings on a behavioral log.
Monitor My Life Satisfaction Behavior – Quotation
Personalize a quotation by stating one's most satisfying past relationships and accomplishments. Identify current and future actions that will contribute to life satisfaction.
Monitor My Hopeful Behavior
Identify a behavioral change and goal related to hope. Document dates, accomplishments, and resultant feelings on a behavioral log.
Monitor My Hopeful Aspects Behavior
Distinguish between aspects of life that are and are not hopeful. Identify ways and list steps to demonstrate greater hope.

Step 6: Reward Myself
Personalize suggestions to buy something affordable or from a resale shop; call or spend time with family or friends; plant seeds; go to a movie, beach or park; sleep late and enjoy a leisurely day.

Step 7: Tips for Motivated Behavior Modification
Acknowledge suggestions in these emotional agility categories: emotions, life satisfaction, and hope.

SUCCESSFUL AGING AND WELL-BEING

EMOTIONAL AGILITY

Step 1: Self-Assessment Introduction and Directions

People who embrace the concept of successful aging acknowledge the need to feel and express positive emotions. A positive emotional outlook allows people to live a satisfying life, think positively about the future, manage negative emotions effectively, and maintain hope for a healthy future.

The *Emotional Agility Self-Assessment* is designed to help you identify your awareness of your emotional outlook. This assessment contains 21 statements that are divided into three areas. Read each of the statements and decide how descriptive the statement is of you. In each of the choices listed, circle the number of your response on the line to the right of each statement.

In the following example, the circled 1 indicates the statement is not at all descriptive of the person completing the inventory:

3 = Like Me   2 = A Little Like Me   1 = Not Like Me

I feel content 3   2   ①

This is not a test and there are no right or wrong answers. Do not spend too much time thinking about your answers. Your initial response will be the most true for you. Be sure to respond to every statement.

SUCCESSFUL AGING AND WELL-BEING

EMOTIONAL AGILITY

Step 1: Self-Assessment

3 = Like Me   2 = A Little Like Me   1 = Not Like Me

I feel content	3	2	1
I have many opportunities	3	2	1
I feel calm	3	2	1
I feel satisfied most of the time	3	2	1
I am encouraged about my future	3	2	1
I feel successful	3	2	1
I feel grateful	3	2	1

F. TOTAL = _____

Some things in my life get better as I get older	3	2	1
I am proud of my age	3	2	1
Life is easy in many ways	3	2	1
I am a wiser person than I used to be	3	2	1
I look back and feel accomplished	3	2	1
I believe that these are good years of my life	3	2	1
As I look back on my life, I am very satisfied	3	2	1

L. TOTAL = _____

I have a positive outlook on life	3	2	1
I have plans for the future	3	2	1
I see the possibilities in situations	3	2	1
I am grateful every day	3	2	1
I look forward to so much in the future	3	2	1
I believe that each day has potential for me	3	2	1
I still feel I have something to contribute to others	3	2	1

H. TOTAL = _____

SUCCESSFUL AGING AND WELL-BEING

EMOTIONAL AGILITY

Step 1: Self-Assessment Scoring Directions

To age successfully, you need to have positive emotions, a sense of meaning and usefulness, and hope for the future. The self-assessment you just completed is designed to help you explore how well you are functioning emotionally. For each of the three sections on the previous page, count the scores you circled. Put that total on the line marked TOTAL at the end of each section. Then, transfer your totals to the spaces below and add your three scores to get your Grand Total:

F. Feelings   Total = _____
L. Life Satisfaction Total = _____
H. Hope   Total = _____
         GRAND TOTAL = _____

Profile Interpretation

Individual Scores	Grand Total	Result	Indications
17 to 21	50 to 63	High	If you scored between 17 and 21 on any assessment, you are functioning well emotionally.
12 to 16	35 to 49	Moderate	If you scored between 12 and 16 on any assessment, you are functioning fairly well emotionally.
7 to 11	21 to 34	Low	If you scored between 7 and 11 on any assessment, you rarely function well emotionally.

Self-Assessment Descriptions

EMOTIONS – People scoring high on this self-assessment feel good about themselves and their future, are satisfied, and do not experience anger and irritation very often.

LIFE SATISFACTION – People scoring high on this self-assessment are satisfied with their lives, feel useful, and are satisfied when looking back over their lives.

HOPE – People scoring high on this self-assessment have a positive outlook on life, are hopeful about their futures, and see each day as providing new opportunities.

GRAND TOTAL – People scoring high on the total of the three self-assessments have positive emotions, a sense of meaning and usefulness, and a strong, positive hope for their future.

SUCCESSFUL AGING AND WELL-BEING

EMOTIONAL AGILITY

Step 2: Recognize and Develop a Support System

In order to feel satisfied with your life and have hope for the future, it is helpful to have people who will support you and be available to you when you need them. Not every person in your life will be helpful for each of your challenges. Complete the following table with people who might be able to support you to maintain positive emotions and an optimistic attitude.

Supporter	How This Person Can Support Me	How I Can Contact This Person
Example: My Friend James	He always sees the positive side of a situation and he can help me do that.	Phone only: 123-456-7890

Keep this list handy. Call, email or text when you need support.

SUCCESSFUL AGING AND WELL-BEING

EMOTIONAL AGILITY

Step 3: Feelings Journaling

Reflecting on and journaling about how you feel as you age can be very valuable. Following are some journaling questions that can help you think about the benefits of maintaining a positive attitude. Remember, successful aging is directly related to your life satisfaction, hope about the future, and maintaining positive emotions.

What do you feel good about in your life right now? _____

_____

_____

What don't you feel good about in your life right now? _____

_____

_____

When you look back over your life, what satisfies you the most? _____

_____

_____

What do you look forward to now? _____

_____

_____

What about your future life concerns you? _____

_____

_____

> *The best and most beautiful things in the world cannot be seen or even touched. They must be felt with the heart.*
>
> ~ Helen Keller

Which best and most beautiful things in your life are felt with your heart?

_____

_____

_____

SUCCESSFUL AGING AND WELL-BEING

EMOTIONAL AGILITY

Step 4: Set Goals

A well-conceived action plan will help to motivate you as you progress in maintaining positive, hopeful, and satisfying emotions. For this activity, identify goals you have for regulating your feelings, life satisfaction, and hope in your aging process. These are goals you can work toward, and when completed, will motivate you to do even more! Complete the action plan below, noting the SMART steps required to reach your goals.

Goals need to be SMART:
Specific, **M**easureable, **A**ttainable, **R**ealistic, and **T**ime-Specific

Goals	How I Will Measure This Goal	How This Goal is Attainable and Realistic	Time Deadline	How This Will Help Me
Example: *To feel more satisfied about the life I lead.*	*The times I feel happy versus sad.*	*I think I have plenty of opportunities to do so.*	*End of the year.*	*I will feel better about my life.*

If you are having trouble identifying goals, consult TIPS, page 46.

SUCCESSFUL AGING AND WELL-BEING

EMOTIONAL AGILITY

Step 5: Monitor My Emotions Behavior

People who are aging successfully experience a wide variety of emotions and are content with their lives most of the time. Periodic re-evaluations support your efforts to continue developing positive emotions about life. Once you reach your goal(s), set new ones to improve or maintain what you have already achieved. Use a separate page for each change.

EXAMPLE:

My emotions behavior change *Worry less about assisted living options as I age.*

My goal *To feel like I have a safe and secure place to live when I get older.*

Date	My Accomplishment	How It Felt
July 26	I made arrangements to visit a few senior living communities in my area.	Now that I know my options, I feel more settled about my future!

✂ -

Healthy Emotions

My emotions behavior change _____

My goal _____

Date	My Accomplishment	How It Felt

SUCCESSFUL AGING AND WELL-BEING

EMOTIONAL AGILITY

Step 5: Monitor My Positive and Negative Emotions Behavior

It's time to explore your current positive and negative emotions you have about your life.

In the table below, identify your positive emotions. *(i.e., confident, content, curious, enthusiastic, ecstatic, excited, happy, hopeful, interested, loved, optimistic, peaceful, proud, relieved, satisfied, etc.)*

My Positive Emotions	What I Am Positive About	What Keeps me Positive

In the table below, identify your **negative emotions**. *(i.e., aggressive, angry, anxious, apathetic, discouraged, envious, helpless, humiliated, hurt, lonely, miserable, paranoid, sad, stubborn, withdrawn, etc.)*

My Negative Emotions	What I Am Negative About	How I Can Start Seeing things in a More Positive Way

Which table was hardest to complete and why? _____

SUCCESSFUL AGING AND WELL-BEING

EMOTIONAL AGILITY

Step 5: Monitor My Life Satisfaction Behavior

People who are aging successfully experience a great deal of life satisfaction. Monitoring the ways you treat people will help to ensure you continue to do so. Keeping track of your interactions will help you determine what you have accomplished and what you need to continue to work on. Periodic re-evaluations support your success, improve or maintain what you have already achieved, and motivate you. Use a separate page for each change.

EXAMPLE:

My life satisfaction behavior change <u>To feel more useful than I do now.</u>

My goal <u>Volunteer at a school.</u>

Date	My Accomplishment	How It Felt
Aug. 14	I started volunteering yesterday at a local school.	Wonderful! I love being with children.

✂ -

Life Satisfaction

My life satisfaction behavior change _____

My goal _____

Date	My Accomplishment	How It Felt

SUCCESSFUL AGING AND WELL-BEING

EMOTIONAL AGILITY

Step 5: Monitor My Life Satisfaction Behavior – Quotation

> *To be able to look back upon one's life in satisfaction, is to live twice.*
> ~Khalil Gibran

What does the above quotation mean to you?
_____
_____
_____
_____

When you look back, which relationships have satisfied you the most?
_____
_____
_____
_____

When you look back, what work or volunteer accomplishment satisfied you the most?
_____
_____
_____
_____

What do you do now that gives you satisfaction?
_____
_____
_____
_____

What can you do in the future that will give you satisfaction?
_____
_____
_____
_____

SUCCESSFUL AGING AND WELL-BEING

EMOTIONAL AGILITY

Step 5: Monitor My Hopeful Behavior

People who age successfully see a bright future that is full of hope regardless of the chronological age. Use the following chart to monitor your progress toward your goals, reinforce your behavior, and determine what you have accomplished at given times. Periodic re-evaluations will help you create new goals for remaining hopeful about the future. Once you reach your goal(s), set new ones to improve or maintain what you have already achieved. Use a separate page for each change.

EXAMPLE:

My hopeful behavior change *To envision a future for myself where I can be as independent as possible.*

My goal *Talk with all of my children and grandchildren about my moving into a smaller place.*

Date	My Accomplishment	How It Felt
Sept. 12	I am researching my options, one by one.	It was comforting to know I had good choices.

✂ -

Hopeful

My hopeful behavior change _____

My goal _____

Date	My Accomplishment	How It Felt

SUCCESSFUL AGING AND WELL-BEING

EMOTIONAL AGILITY

Step 5: Monitor My Hopeful Aspects Behavior

Consider the many aspects of life about which you can be hopeful, even if there other aspects that are not hopeful. In the spaces that follow, explore the things about which you are hopeful and those that you are not hopeful about.

Hopeful Aspects of My Life
Example: *My granddaughter is engaged.*
_____
_____
_____
_____
_____
_____

Not So Hopeful Aspects of My Life
My health
_____
_____
_____
_____
_____
_____

Now take some of the items in the "Not So Hopeful" column and find ways to be more optimistic and proactive.

Not So Hopeful	Ways I Can Be More Hopeful	Steps I Can Take to Accomplish This
Example: My health.	I can find a medical professional with whom I feel confident.	I can listen carefully and do what this person suggests.

SUCCESSFUL AGING AND WELL-BEING

EMOTIONAL AGILITY

Step 6: Reward Myself

As you age, it is important to remain hopeful and upbeat about your future. When you succeed in being more positive and hopeful you need to reward yourself! For some people, it may seem awkward to reward yourself, however, you will find that you are more likely to repeat behaviors if you find a way to give yourself a reward. Your reward should give you the incentive to achieve your goals. It should be within your budget and something you'll be excited about. If it involves money, be sure your reward is something you wouldn't ordinarily buy or do.

Some possible rewards might include:
- Buy something that will make your life more enjoyable.
- Call someone you haven't spoken to in ages.
- Plant seeds in a pot.
- See a movie in the middle of the day.
- Sit in a park or at the beach.
- Sleep in until noon, have a leisurely lunch and do nothing for the rest of the day.
- Spend the day with a friend or family member you rarely get to see.
- Visit a resale shop with a budget of five dollars.

Now list five rewards that you will give yourself when you achieve a goal:

1._____

2._____

3._____

4._____

5._____

You deserve a pat on the back for the good work you are completing in this section. Rewards help you to pay attention to your triumphs, not your setbacks. Rewards will create good feelings and propel you to want to work harder to reach your goals.

Whenever you have completed or achieved one of your goals, treat yourself to one of the items on your list

SUCCESSFUL AGING AND WELL-BEING

EMOTIONAL AGILITY

Step 7: Tips For Motivated Behavior Modifications

EMOTIONS
- Be aware of the symptoms of depression. As people age, they may feel sad about the past and worried about the future. If you are experiencing these symptoms, consult a medical practitioner.
- Carefully examine the events that bring on negative emotions. Examine ways to avoid these situations or reframe them so that they are less emotional.
- Find ways to diffuse your negative emotions, or even laugh at the absurdity of certain situations.
- Remember that your thoughts often trigger certain negative emotions.
- Switch from negative self-talk to positive self-talk to boost yourself up.

LIFE SATISFACTION
- Become involved with a spiritual or religious community.
- Continue to set goals for yourself. These goals can be related to your personal, social, volunteer, or professional life.
- Keep growing. Visit new places, learn new things, and engage in new experiences.
- Maintain and keep old friends whose company you enjoy.
- Make new friends with whom you can share time and stories.
- Write your life story and include all of the aspects that have made you proud over the years.

HOPE
- Be playful and open to new possibilities. Feel hopeful about exploring and attaining these new possibilities.
- Make a list of possibilities.
- Begin to plan and achieve short and long-term goals to change what you can.
- New experiences allow you to use your imagination and creativity. You might discover additional ways to make your life better.
- Regret can produce a pattern of negative thinking about your life. Remember that the past cannot be changed, and you possibly did the best you could at that time. Focus on the present and future.

SECTION III

HEALTHY LIFESTYLE

*The root of all evil is in the brain.
The trunk of it is in emotion.
The branches and the leaves are the body.
The flower of health blooms when all parts work together.*

– **Kurdish saying**

Name _____

Date _____

SUCCESSFUL AGING AND WELL-BEING

HEALTHY LIFESTYLE

Section I: Skills Emphasized in Each Activity Handout

Step 1: Self-Assessment
Respond to a set of prompts, self-score, and interpret personal profile on three scales: sleep, exercise, and nutrition.

Step 2: Recognize and Develop a Support System
Identify possible healthy lifestyle supporters, types of support they can provide, and their contact information.

Step 3: Healthy Lifestyle Journaling
Evaluate current health and aspects to improve. Describe one's nutritional and sleep habits. Document types and frequency of exercise. Identify ways to improve health that are under personal control.

Step 4: Set Goals
Set goals that are specific, measureable, attainable, realistic, and time-specific. Identify ways to improve and maintain health. Note how these goals enhance successful aging.

Step 5: Monitor My Sleep Behavior
Identify a behavioral change and goal related to sleep. Document dates, accomplishments, and resultant feelings on a behavioral log.

Monitor My Sleep Behavior – Rating
Rate suggestions on ten point scale. State ways to implement suggestions rated three or above.

Monitor My Exercise Behavior
Identify a behavioral change and goal related to exercise. Document dates, accomplishments, and resultant feelings on a behavioral log.

Monitor My Form of Exercise Behavior
Respond to a list of suggestions, noting how to engage in each form of exercise and possible barriers. Select preferred forms of exercise and list the steps to get started.

Monitor My Nutrition Behavior
Identify a behavioral change and goal related to nutrition. Document dates, accomplishments, and resultant feelings on a behavioral log.

Monitor My Nutrition Habits Behavior
Respond to a list of suggestions, noting how they improve health and ways to overcome obstacles.

Step 6: Reward Myself
Personalize a quotation by identifying an accomplishment that helped one pause, reflect, and relish success. Note how life is different due to the accomplishment. Describe rewards that motivate one to develop a healthy lifestyle.

Step 7: Tips for Motivated Behavior Modification
Acknowledge suggestions in these healthy lifestyle categories: sleep, exercise, and nutrition.

SUCCESSFUL AGING AND WELL-BEING

HEALTHY LIFESTYLE

Step 1: Self-Assessment Introduction and Directions

Living a healthy life brings many rewards. People who age successfully will have more energy, become more fit, and live well longer by developing and maintaining a healthy lifestyle. A healthy lifestyle can also help to increase self-esteem, and ensure a positive mental outlook.

The *Healthy Lifestyle Self-Assessment* is designed to raise your awareness of your current lifestyle. This self-assessment contains 30 statements that are divided into three lifestyle categories. Read each of the statements and decide the extent to which the statement describes you. Circle the number of your response on the line to the right of each statement.

In the following example, the circled 3 indicates the statement is usually like the person completing the self-assessment:

Do not pay attention to the numbers, just these headings:

- **Usually like me**
- **Not usually like me**
- **Not like me**

	Usually Like Me	Not Usually Like Me	Not Like Me
For my age ...			
I get enough sleep every night	(3)	2	1

This is not a test and there are no right or wrong answers. Do not spend too much time thinking about your answers. Your initial response will be the most true for you. Be sure to respond to every statement.

SUCCESSFUL AGING AND WELL-BEING

HEALTHY LIFESTYLE

Step 1: Self-Assessment

	Usually Like Me	Not Usually Like Me	Not Like Me
FOR MY AGE ...			
I get enough sleep every night	3	2	1
I am rarely irritable from a lack of sleep	3	2	1
I have a regular sleep routine	3	2	1
I nap several times during the day	1	2	3
I can do okay with less than eight hours of sleep per night	3	2	1
I have fallen asleep while in the middle of something	1	2	3
I feel fatigued a lot of the time	1	2	3
I take a short nap during the day if I need to	3	2	1
I have difficulty falling asleep	1	2	3
Any noise or movement keeps me awake at night	1	2	3

S. TOTAL = _____

I do not keep myself fit	1	2	3
Taking care of my body is important to me	3	2	1
I make an effort to stay physically active	3	2	1
I am proud of how I look and feel	3	2	1
I don't walk very much	1	2	3
I take time to exercise regularly	3	2	1
I don't make time to exercise	1	2	3
I have a long-term exercise plan I stick to	3	2	1
I set aside a regular time for exercising	3	2	1
I use the proper equipment when I exercise	3	2	1

E. TOTAL = _____

I maintain my appropriate weight	3	2	1
I eat fresh fruits and vegetables every day	3	2	1
I have irregular and inconsistent eating habits	1	2	3
Whenever possible, I minimize salt (sodium) intake	3	2	1
I am conscious of my cholesterol and fat intake	3	2	1
I minimize sugar in my snacks and meals	3	2	1
I consume way too many calories	1	2	3
I like my "fast foods"	1	2	3
I often eat too much food at meals	1	2	3
I consume more alcohol than the doctor would suggest	1	2	3

N. TOTAL = _____

SUCCESSFUL AGING AND WELL-BEING

HEALTHY LIFESTYLE

Step 1: Self-Assessment Scoring Directions

A healthy lifestyle goes a long way to help with successful aging. For each of the three sections on the previous page, total the scores you circled. Put that total on the line marked TOTAL at the end of each section. Then, transfer your totals to the spaces below and add the three scores to get your Grand Total:

    S. Sleep   Total = _____

    E. Exercise   Total = _____

    N. Nutrition   Total = _____

    GRAND TOTAL = _____

Profile Interpretation

Individual Scores	Grand Total	Result	Indications
24 to 30	71 to 90	High	You are living a very healthy lifestyle in this time of your life.
17 to 23	51 to 70	Moderate	You are living a fairly healthy lifestyle in this time of your life.
10 to 16	30 to 50	Low	You are not living a very healthy lifestyle in this time of your life.

Self-Assessment Descriptions

SLEEP – People who score high on this self-assessment tend to sleep well and have a regular sleep routine in order to maintain a healthy lifestyle.

EXERCISE – People who score high on this self-assessment tend to be engaging in adequate amounts of exercise in order to maintain a healthy lifestyle.

NUTRITION – People who score high on this self-assessment tend to be eating proper foods in order to maintain a healthy lifestyle.

GRAND TOTAL – People who score high on all three self-assessments enjoy and maintain a healthy lifestyle.

SUCCESSFUL AGING AND WELL-BEING

HEALTHY LIFESTYLE

Step 2: Recognize and Develop a Support System

As people age it can become more of a challenge to maintain a healthy lifestyle. It can become more difficult to have a healthy food plan, get enough exercise, and sleep well. To do so, you need the support of people who can help. Not every supportive person in your life will be helpful with every area of your life. Complete the following table with people you think might be able to support you with your efforts to live a healthier lifestyle.

Supporter	How This Person Can Support Me	How I Can Contact This Person
Example: My friend RD	*When she goes to the health club three or four times a week, she can take me.*	*Phone or text: 000-000-0001, email: rd@.com.*

Keep this list handy. Call, email or text when you need support.

SUCCESSFUL AGING AND WELL-BEING

HEALTHY LIFESTYLE

Step 3: Healthly Lifestyle Journaling

Journaling is an excellent way to truly look at the ways you are maintaining a healthy lifestyle. The questions that follow have been designed to help you think with an open mind about your current lifestyles. Respond to the following journaling questions.

How would you describe your current state of health? _____
_____
_____

What can you do to improve your health? _____
_____
_____

What aspects of your life do you think are healthy? Which are not? _____
_____
_____

What are your eating habits? Are they healthy or not? _____
_____
_____

What are your sleeping habits and how effective are they? _____
_____
_____

What types of exercise do you do, and how often do you engage in each form of exercise? _____
_____
_____

What is under your control to change, so that you can be even healthier than you are currently?
_____
_____

SUCCESSFUL AGING AND WELL-BEING

HEALTHY LIFESTYLE

Step 4: Set Goals

In order to experience a healthy lifestyle, you will need to develop goals to improve your sleep, exercise and nutrition routines. This will ensure that you remain motivated in your efforts to learn, practice and maintain effective skills. These are goals you can work toward, and when completed, will motivate you to do even more! Complete the action plan below, noting the SMART steps required to reach your goals.

Goals need to be SMART:

Specific, **M**easureable, **A**ttainable, **R**ealistic, and **T**ime-Specific

Goals	How I Will Measure This Goal	How This Goal is Attainable and Realistic	Time Deadline	How This Will Help Me
Example: To lose 50 pounds.	Weigh myself each day and lose at least 2 pounds a week.	Yes, I will cut down on late-night desserts and start exercising.	A year from now.	My back will feel SO much better and my blood test results will improve.

If you are having trouble identifying goals, consult TIPS, page 62.

SUCCESSFUL AGING AND WELL-BEING

HEALTHY LIFESTYLE

Step 5: Monitor My Sleep Behavior

A full night's sleep sounds easy, but can be more difficult as people age. There are some simple ways that you can start benefitting from a better night's sleep. The table below will help you keep track of your sleep goals. Identify some goals and then periodically re-evaluate them. Once you reach your goal(s), set new ones to improve or maintain what you have already achieved. Use a separate page for each change.

EXAMPLE:

My sleep behavior change   To take fewer naps during the day.

My goal   To sleep better at night.

Date	My Accomplishment	How It Felt
Oct. 13	I slept 8 hours a night for a week.	I feel alert during the day.

- -

Sleep

My healthy sleep behavior change _____

My goal _____

Date	My Accomplishment	How It Felt

SUCCESSFUL AGING AND WELL-BEING

HEALTHY LIFESTYLE

Step 5: Monitor My Sleep Behavior - Rating

Complete the table below to help you identify the ways you can ensure better sleep. In the second column, rate the suggestion, from **0 = Not for Me, to 10 = Great Idea, I'll try it!** If you rate the suggestion 3 or more, fill out the next column.

Suggestions	Rate this Suggestion 0 to 10	How I Can Make This a Regular Part of My Routine
The bedroom is for sleep or sex only. No reading, TV, tablet, games, etc.		
Have a regular sleep schedule, waking up the same time every morning.		
Move clocks out of view.		
Relax before bedtime. (bath, shower, music, meditation, guided imagery)		
Find the right number of hours you need to sleep and work to do that regularly.		
Avoid exercise or heavy eating 3-4 hours before bedtime.		
Have no lights on during sleep other than a night light.		
Sleep 7 to 9 hours each night.		
Have a pre-bedtime routine. (bath, book, music, non-violent TV)		
Enjoy some sunlight every day.		
No caffeine or alcohol late in the day.		
Eat large meals at lunch, rather than dinner.		

Which of the above sleep routines do you want to begin doing immediately?

SUCCESSFUL AGING AND WELL-BEING

HEALTHY LIFESTYLE

Step 5: Monitor My Exercise Behavior

Some form of exercise is critical in any healthy lifestyle plan. You will need to think of the types of exercise appropriate for you. The table below will help you keep track of your exercise goals. Identify some goals and then periodically re-evaluate them. Once you reach your goal(s), set new ones to improve or maintain what you have already achieved. Use a separate page for each change.

EXAMPLE:

My exercise behavior change To walk more than once a week.

My goal To walk a mile three times per week.

Date	My Accomplishment	How It Felt
August 30	Walked a half a mile twice this week.	Felt great - lots more energy.

✂ -

Exercise

My healthy exercise behavior change _____

My goal _____

Date	My Accomplishment	How It Felt

SUCCESSFUL AGING AND WELL-BEING

HEALTHY LIFESTYLE

Step 5: Monitor My Form of Exercise Behavior

Any type of exercise is better than no exercise!

Forms of Exercise	How I Can Do This	What Stops Me
Dancing / Zumba		
Gym/Fitness Center (treadmill, elliptical machine, stationary bike, rowing machine)		
Local mall walking Walk outside Walk a dog		
Swim laps Water aerobics		
Tennis / Bocce ball / Bowling		
Use soup cans as weights to strengthen arms		
Walk around a museum or shopping mall		
Yoga / Tai Chi / Martial arts		
Other		

Which of the above ways of exercising are you ready to start? _____

_____

_____

_____

Describe the steps you will take to start. _____

_____

_____

_____

SUCCESSFUL AGING AND WELL-BEING

HEALTHY LIFESTYLE

Step 5: Monitor My Nutrition Behavior

Nutrition is necessary in maintaining a healthy lifestyle. Think about, write down, and then monitor your goals for achieving proper nutrition habits in your healthy lifestyle. Don't forget to periodically re-evaluate them and once you reach your personal life goal(s), set new ones to improve or maintain what you have already achieved. Use a separate page for each change.

EXAMPLE:

My nutrition behavior change   Eat more meals at home where I can control what I eat and what is in the food.

My goal   Consume the recommended types and amounts of food and liquid.

Date	My Accomplishment	How It Felt
June 15	I went out only once and it wasn't fast food.	Proud of myself.

Nutrition

My nutrition behavior change _____

My goal _____

Date	My Accomplishment	How It Felt

SUCCESSFUL AGING AND WELL-BEING

HEALTHY LIFESTYLE

Step 5: Monitor My Nutritional Habits Behavior

Complete the table to help you identify the types of nutritional habits you want or need to change based on any medical suggestions and/or restrictions.

Nutritional Habits	How This Will Help Me to Be Healthier	Obstacles	How I can Overcome the Obstacles
Example: Less sugar	It will help my high sugar count and my weight.	Everywhere I go people serve things with sugar.	I can bring my own sugar free dessert or fruit.
Less sugar			
Lots of fruits and vegetables			
Whole grain breads			
Drink a lot of water before becoming thirsty			
Reduce overall fat content			
Reduce caffeine and alcohol			
Other			
Other			
Other			
Other			
Other			

SUCCESSFUL AGING AND WELL-BEING

HEALTHY LIFESTYLE

Step 6: Reward Myself

In society today, it can be difficult to develop and maintain a healthy lifestyle, and when you do, you deserve a reward! But what type of reward would keep you motivated? The answer to this question will be different for each person.

Your reward needs to be something that will give you the incentive to achieve your goals. It needs to be within your budget and something you'll be excited about. If you are buying yourself something, be sure your reward is something you wouldn't ordinarily buy or do. Remember that some of the best things in life are free.

Think about the following quote:

> *Celebrating your accomplishments, or acknowledging them, or rewarding yourself for what you've achieved helps you to pause, reflect, and take time to relish what you've accomplished, and how your life might be different as a result.*
>
> ~Khalil Gibran

What does this quote mean to you? _____
_____
_____

How have your accomplishments helped you to pause and reflect? _____
_____
_____

How is your life different because of what you have accomplished? _____
_____
_____

How can you relish your accomplishments? _____
_____
_____

What rewards would motivate you as you take steps in developing a healthy life style? ___
_____
_____
_____

SUCCESSFUL AGING AND WELL-BEING

HEALTHY LIFESTYLE

Step 7: Tips For Motivated Behavior Modifications

Sleep
- Develop a regular evening ritual that allows you to slow down and release any worries and anxieties you may have. Some ways to do this include prayer, meditation, and deep breathing exercises.
- Do not do exercises that make you sweat before bedtime.
- Establish a standard wake-up time to set your circadian rhythms and to train yourself to stay on a schedule even though you might not have to get up at a certain time.
- Have no laptops, technology or televisions in your bedroom. These types of stimuli will keep you awake.
- If you need some sort of background noise, machines or CDs are available to provide noise such as ocean waves or rain. This "noise" will drown out any things that might keep you awake.
- Make sure your room is cool and dark.
- Refrain from using alcohol or nicotine a couple of hours before bedtime.
- The bedroom is for sleep and/or sex only.

Exercise
- Attend classes for a light cardio workout such as Chi-gong, or Tai Chi.
- Exercising strengthens and stretches your muscles which can be beneficial by helping you maintain a healthy weight and build stronger bones.
- Find a friend with whom to exercise.
- If you are physically able, train for resistance by using barbells, exercise machines, dumbbells, and resistance bands.
- Integrate exercise and activity into your daily lifestyle.
- Join a gym or senior center that offers all types of exercise, including chair and wheelchair exercises.
- Play games that allow you to engage in some exercise.
- Use non-traditional methods to exercise such as dancing or water aerobics.
- Walk, do calisthenics, jog, or hike to increase your overall mobility and endurance.

Nutrition
- Attend a nutrition program and enjoy meals in the community.
- Drink plenty of water to stop hunger pangs, fight bad breath and avoid dry mouth.
- Eat a healthy lunch in the park.
- Sit by a window and enjoy a nutritious meal. Use your best tableware.
- Invite a friend to a potluck dinner.
- Make leftovers into "planned leftovers."
- Prepare a new healthy recipe and invite friends over for a tasting party.
- Treat yourself to a meal out.
- Use vitamin supplements as recommended by your physician. These supplements can supply minerals and nutrients that may not be sufficient in your diet.

SECTION IV

DAILY LIVING

*Aging is not lost youth,
but a new stage of opportunity and strength.*

– Betty Friedan

Name_____

Date_____

DAILY LIVING

Section I: Skills Emphasized in Each Activity Handout

Step 1: Self-Assessment
Respond to a set of prompts, self-score, and interpret personal profile on four scales: worry, spirituality, medical, and self-care.

Step 2: Recognize and Develop a Support System
Identify possible daily living supporters, types of support they can provide, and their contact information.

Step 3: Daily Living Journaling
Describe worries, medical situation, ability to care for self, and ways one finds meaning in life.

Step 4: Set Goals
Set goals that are specific, measureable, attainable, realistic, and time-specific. Identify ways to improve and maintain daily living skills. Note how these goals enhance successful aging.

Step 5: Monitor My Worry Behavior
Identify a behavioral change and goal related to worry. Document dates, accomplishments, and resultant feelings on a behavioral log.

Monitor My Spirituality Behavior
Identify a behavioral change and goal related to spirituality. Document dates, accomplishments, and resultant feelings on a behavioral log.

Monitor My Medical Behavior
Identify a behavioral change and goal related to medical issues. Document dates, accomplishments, and resultant feelings on a behavioral log.

Monitor My Self-Care Behavior
Identify a behavioral change and goal related to self-care. Document dates, accomplishments, and resultant feelings on a behavioral log.

Monitor My Daily Living Behavior
Describe verbally and/or graphically what life will be like when daily living goals are achieved in each of these areas: worry, spirituality, medical, and self-care.

Step 6: Reward Myself
Identify rewards that are exciting, meaningful, small, large, free, affordable, can be enjoyed alone, and can be enjoyed with others. Use the set of affirmations provided as rewards. Cut them out and post in prominent places.

Step 7: Tips for Motivated Behavior Modification
Acknowledge suggestions in these daily living categories: worry, spirituality, medical, and self-care.

SUCCESSFUL AGING AND WELL-BEING

DAILY LIVING

Step 1: Self-Assessment Introduction and Directions

Operating and functioning on a daily basis can become more of a challenge as people get older. They may experience new medical issues, have difficulty taking care of themselves, worry, feel depressed, and have questions related to meaning and purpose in later life.

The *Daily Living Self-Assessment* is designed to help you explore how well you are functioning. This assessment contains 24 statements. Read each of the statements and decide whether or not the statement describes you. If the statement does describe you, circle the YES next to that item. If the statement does not describe you, circle the NO next to that item.

In the following example, the circled number under "Yes" indicates the statement is descriptive of the person completing this self-assessment.

	YES	NO
I do not worry very much about my health	(2)	1

This is not a test. Since there are no right or wrong answers, do not spend too much time thinking about your answers. Be sure to respond to every statement.

SUCCESSFUL AGING AND WELL-BEING

DAILY LIVING

Step 1: Self-Assessment

	YES	NO
I do not worry very much about my health	2	1
I am not concerned over most situations	2	1
I stay calm when I'm under pressure	2	1
I feel sad, but no longer worry too much about family's problems	2	1
I don't get upset about finances	2	1
I don't concern myself about the next phase of life, I just enjoy each day	2	1

A. TOTAL = _____

	YES	NO
My belief system provides me with meaning	2	1
I find strength in my spirituality	2	1
I believe in a Higher Power	2	1
I feel inspired by nature and the wonder of the universe	2	1
I am helped by healing therapists	2	1
I often lean on my faith	2	1

B. TOTAL = _____

	YES	NO
I take my medications	2	1
I understand my health benefits	2	1
I go regularly for medical check-ups	2	1
I have completed a medical power of attorney	2	1
I like my health care team	2	1
I am sure my health professional evaluates the compatibility of my meds	2	1

C. TOTAL = _____

	YES	NO
I can do basic household chores	2	1
I can groom myself	2	1
I can bathe myself	2	1
I can go to the bathroom by myself	2	1
I can dress myself	2	1
I can walk where I need to go	2	1

D. TOTAL = _____

SUCCESSFUL AGING AND WELL-BEING

DAILY LIVING

Step 1: Self-Assessment Scoring Directions

People who age successfully continue to be able to function well on a daily basis. They are prone not to worry too much, have a comfortable belief system, are on top of their health care, and are able to care for themselves.

For each of the four sections on the previous page, total the scores you circled. Put that total on the line marked TOTAL at the end of each section. Then, transfer your totals to the spaces below and add them all for a Grand Total:

> A. Worry   Total = _____
> B. Spirituality   Total = _____
> C. Medical   Total = _____
> D. Self-Care   Total = _____
>   GRAND TOTAL = _____

Profile Interpretation

Individual Scores	Grand Total	Result	Indications
11 to 12	41 to 48	High	You demonstrate many of the behaviors of effective daily functioning.
8 to 10	32 to 40	Moderate	You demonstrate some of the behaviors leading to effective daily functioning.
6 to 7	24 to 31	Low	You do not demonstrate many of the behaviors leading to effective daily functioning.

Self-Assessment Descriptions

WORRY – People scoring high on this assessment do not spend their time and energy worrying about life and death.

SPIRITUALITY – People scoring high on this assessment have a way of tapping into their spirituality.

MEDICAL – People scoring high on this assessment are comfortable with their medical care and practitioners.

SELF-CARE – People scoring high on this assessment successfully care for themselves.

GRAND TOTAL – People scoring high on all four assessments are functioning well in their daily life in the areas of worry, spirituality, medical care, and self-care.

SUCCESSFUL AGING AND WELL-BEING

DAILY LIVING

Step 2: Recognize and Develop a Support System

The way you are able to function on a daily basis has a tremendous effect on whether you age successfully or not. It is important to maintain effective daily functioning. Complete the following table with people who might be able to support you in functioning effectively on a daily basis.

Supporter	How This Person Can Support Me	How I Can Contact This Person
Example: My son	He reminds me to make health care appointments.	Phone 000-000-0000.

Keep this list handy. Call, email or text when you need support.

SUCCESSFUL AGING AND WELL-BEING

DAILY LIVING

Step 3: Daily Living Journaling

Journaling can definitely help you to evaluate how you are functioning. The sentence starters below will help you explore the ways you are functioning in your everyday life.

I worry the most about _____

_____

_____

I worry the least about _____

_____

_____

I wish I could stop worrying about _____

_____

_____

I think my medical situation is _____

_____

_____

My ability to care for myself _____

_____

_____

I find meaning in life _____

_____

_____

SUCCESSFUL AGING AND WELL-BEING

DAILY LIVING

Step 4: Set Goals

In order to function well in your daily life, you need to develop goals related to worrying, belief system, medical care, and self-care. These are goals you can work toward, and when completed, will motivate you to do even more! Complete the action plan below, noting the SMART steps required to reach your goals.

Goals need to be SMART:

Specific, **M**easureable, **A**ttainable, **R**ealistic, and **T**ime-Specific

Goals	How I Will Measure This Goal	How This Goal is Attainable and Realistic	Time Deadline	How This Will Help Me
Example: I want to stop worrying about whether or not to stop working.	When I make a decision.	I will investigate my financial situation and talk to my partner.	2 months.	I can finally relax knowing I've decided when I can retire.

If you are having trouble identifying goals, consult TIPS, page 77.

SUCCESSFUL AGING AND WELL-BEING

DAILY LIVING

Step 5: Monitor My Worry Behavior

Being relatively free of worries is important. We all worry, but we need to be sure we can put each worry in place, stop thinking about it, and let it go. Setting boundary-related goals and monitoring your progress toward those goals will help to reinforce the quality of your daily functioning. The table below will guide you through the development and tracking of these goals. Review your behaviors periodically to ensure you are progressing. Once you reach a goal, set new ones to continue to be worry free. Use a separate page for each change.

EXAMPLE:

My worry behavior change *I will worry less about my grandchild's problems.*

My goal *I want to stay in the present.*

Date	My Accomplishment	How It Felt
April 9	I spent an entire day being mindful of things I love and enjoying every moment.	Relieving. I realized at the end of the day there was nothing I could do by worrying.

Worry

My worry behavior change _____

My goal _____

Date	My Accomplishment	How It Felt

SUCCESSFUL AGING AND WELL-BEING

DAILY LIVING

Step 5: Monitor My Spirituality Behavior

It is important to tap into your own spirituality. Spirituality means something different to everyone. For some, it's about participating in organized religion. For others, it's more personal: some people get in touch with their spiritual side through private prayer, yoga, meditation, quiet reflection, or nature and long walks. Use the table below to set some goals for allowing your spirituality to enhance your daily life. Monitor your behavior to help you determine how successful you have been in doing so. Once you reach your goal(s), set new ones to improve or maintain what you have already achieved. Use a separate page for each change.

EXAMPLE:

My spirituality behavior change   <u>I need to be outside more to spend more time in the awesomeness of nature</u>

My goal   <u>Be outside every day, no matter what the weather, and write what I see.</u>

Date	My Accomplishment	How It Felt
Oct. 30	I talked with seven friends. Each day one is going to call me to tell me to go outside, or go out with me.	I was thrilled when they all said yes, and know it would help them too!

Spirituality

My spirituality behavior change_____

My goal _____

Date	My Accomplishment	How It Felt

SUCCESSFUL AGING AND WELL-BEING

DAILY LIVING

Step 5: Monitor My Medical Behavior

To feel comfortable about your health and health care is critical. In the spaces that follow, identify some of the goals you have for improving your medical situation. Monitoring your progress toward these goals will be helpful. Keep track of your behaviors through the table below, re-evaluate your success, and then set new goals to enhance what you have already achieved. Use a separate page for each change.

EXAMPLE:

My medical behavior change   I want a more empathetic doctor.

My goal   To find a doctor I like and make a change.

Date	My Accomplishment	How It Felt
Oct. 11	I researched doctors in my area and found one I like.	I feel proud of myself and grateful I found her.

Medical

My medical behavior change _____

My goal _____

Date	My Accomplishment	How It Felt

SUCCESSFUL AGING AND WELL-BEING

DAILY LIVING

Step 5: Monitor My Self-Care Behavior

Feeling that you can properly take care of yourself is important to your daily functioning. In the spaces that follow, identify some of the goals you have for improving and maintaining your ability to care for yourself. Monitoring your progress toward these types of goals will help you to age successfully. Keep track of your behaviors with the table below, re-evaluate your success, and then set new goals to enhance what you have already achieved. Use a separate page for each change.

EXAMPLE:

My self-care behavior change *To be able to bathe and groom myself.*

My goal *To be more in control of my self-care.*

Date	My Accomplishment	How It Felt
1/1/2016	I started doing light exercises to build my strength.	I feel empowered because I am slowly regaining my strength and doing more on my own.

Self-Care

My self-care behavior change _____

My goal _____

Date	My Accomplishment	How It Felt

SUCCESSFUL AGING AND WELL-BEING

DAILY LIVING

Step 5: Monitor My Daily Living Behavior

In the spaces that follow, write about, or draw, what your life will be like when you achieve your daily living goals

Worry …	Spirituality …
Medical …	Self-Care …

SUCCESSFUL AGING AND WELL-BEING

DAILY LIVING

Step 6: Reward Myself

The ability to function independently each day can usually be attained and will help you to age successfully. There are specific ways to do this, and you have learned many of them in this section. As you complete goals and find yourself functioning more effectively, you need to reward yourself. Your rewards need to be something that will give you the incentive to achieve even more goals. They need to be within your budget and something you'll be excited about. If you are buying yourself something, be certain that your reward is something you wouldn't ordinarily buy or do.

Brainstorm possible rewards.

- Rewards that would be meaningful to me _____
- Small rewards I could give myself _____
- Large rewards I could give myself _____
- Things that would not cost money and that would be fun _____
- Rewards I can afford and that would be fun _____
- Rewards that I can enjoy alone _____
- Rewards I can enjoy with people who support me _____

You deserve a pat on the back for the good work you are completing in this section. Rewards help you to pay attention to your triumphs, not your setbacks. Rewards will create good feelings and propel you to want to work harder to reach your goals. Whenever you have completed or achieved one of your goals, treat yourself to one of the items on your list.

You can also reward yourself by giving yourself positive affirmations when achieving a goal. Below are some samples. Cut them out and post in visible spots everywhere! If these don't work for your goal, write your own on sticky notes!

I lovingly take care of my body!	My chronological age is merely a number	People get better with age
YAY! GOOD FOR ME!	I'm thrilled to be aging as well as I am!	I grow wiser as I age!
Aging can be fun!	I appreciate life more than I did yesterday!	I am not afraid of aging!
I like gray hair! I earned it!	PEOPLE DO NOT AGE ... THEY MATURE!	I am the perfect age today!

SUCCESSFUL AGING AND WELL-BEING

DAILY LIVING

Step 7: Tips For Motivated Behavior Modifications

Worry
- Use meditation to clear your mind. One way to do so is to count your breaths. This will be difficult at first as your mind will jump from thought to thought. When this happens, simply make note of the thought and return to counting your breaths.
- Don't try to control things you cannot control in life.
- Live in the moment. Stop regretting aspects of your past. They have happened and you cannot change them. Stop obsessing about the future because it is not here yet.
- Practice self-acceptance. Accept yourself as you currently are.
- Count your blessings. Focus on all that you have accomplished as a human being.

Spirituality
- Try practicing meditation, yoga, deep breathing, praying and other methods for quieting your mind to help you make greater spiritual connections.
- If it sounds like a good idea, explore ways that you can connect with a Higher Power. This might include identifying a house of worship that feels comfortable to you.
- Walk outside, close your eyes, and smell the air. Open your eyes and look around. Listen to the birds. Allow yourself to feel what you feel.

Medical
- Find a physician or medical team that you like and is empathetic to your medical needs. Be sure all members of the team have each other's contact information to know everything going on with you.
- Schedule regular physical and mental health, dental, vision, auditory, dermatology, and any other medical specialist check-ups as applicable to you, as needed.
- Make medical appointments as preventative measures to catch issues before they become problems.
- Do research and investigate medical benefits that are available to you.

Self-Care
- If you need assistance, seek help from other people. They may be friends, family, medical professionals, etc.
- Get enough sleep and begin a gentle exercise routine to build muscle.
- Identify living centers staffed with people who can help you with self-care.
- Install enhancements and equipment in your home that can help you care for yourself.
- Eat and drink nutritiously. Your body will thank you for it!

SECTION V
SENSE OF HUMOR

*You may not be able to change a situation,
but with humor you can change your attitude about it.*

– Allen Klein

Name_____

Date_____

SUCCESSFUL AGING AND WELL-BEING

SENSE OF HUMOR

Section I: Skills Emphasized in Each Activity Handout

Step 1: Self-Assessment
Respond to a set of prompts, self-score, and interpret personal profile on a sense of humor scale.

Step 2: Recognize and Develop a Support System
Identify possible sense of humor supporters, types of support they can provide, and their contact information.

Step 3: Sense of Humor Journaling
Share situations in which one does and does not like to laugh at self, and situations in which one will and will not laugh at others. Describe situations in which a sense of humor helps and what it allows one to do.

Step 4: Set Goals
Set goals that are specific, measureable, attainable, realistic, and time-specific. Identify ways to improve and maintain daily living skills. Note how these goals enhance successful aging.

Step 5: Monitor My Humor Behavior
Identify a behavioral change and goal related to sense of humor. Document dates, accomplishments, and resultant feelings on a behavioral log.

Monitor My Laughter Behavior
List humorous movies, TV programs, books, people, situations, activities, stories, etc. Select the most humorous in each category and describe how one is affected by each type of humor.

Sense of Humor Quotation
Personalize a quotation by stating how one's sense of humor provides armor and a good grasp of life. Describe the joy in one's heart.

Step 6: Reward Myself
Reward self by reviewing the extensive list of life's bonuses that result from the ability to laugh.

Step 7: Tips for Motivated Behavior Modification
Acknowledge suggestions to incorporate laughter into daily life.

SUCCESSFUL AGING AND WELL-BEING

SENSE OF HUMOR

Step 1: Self-Assessment Introduction and Directions

It is important to maintain a healthy sense of humor, especially as we are getting older. When humor and laughter are shared, they bind people together socially and protect people from the various sources of stress.

The *Sense of Humor Self-Assessment* will help you explore the strength of your sense of humor.

This assessment contains 20 statements that explore how well you are maintaining a sense of humor in your life. Read each of the statements and decide whether or not the statement describes you. If the statement does describe you, circle the number in the YES column. If the statement does not describe you, circle the number in the NO column.

In the following example, the circled number under YES indicates the statement is descriptive of the person completing the inventory

	YES	NO
I am able to laugh at myself	(2)	1

This is not a test and there are no right or wrong answers. Do not spend too much time thinking about your answers. Your initial response will be the most true for you. Be sure to respond to every statement.

SUCCESSFUL AGING AND WELL-BEING

SENSE OF HUMOR

Step 1: Self-Assessment

	YES	NO
I am able to laugh at myself	2	1
I don't like to share embarrassing moments	1	2
I take myself too seriously	1	2
I often find absurdity in serious situations	2	1
I enjoy good jokes	2	1
I smile a lot	2	1
I tell appropriate jokes	2	1
I enjoy hearing funny stories	2	1
I am unable to bring positive humor into my conversations	1	2
I try to lighten up in most situations	2	1
I look for humor in negative situations	2	1
I like to spend time with fun-loving, playful people	2	1
I like to do silly things	2	1
I do not enjoy funny movies or television shows	1	2
I rarely laugh	1	2
I enjoy playing with children	2	1
I would not enjoy going to a comedy club	1	2
I enjoy reading fun books, magazines and/or newspaper comics	2	1
I wish I enjoyed a more playful sense of humor	1	2
I still see humor in a difficult situation	2	1

TOTAL = _____

SUCCESSFUL AGING AND WELL-BEING

SENSE OF HUMOR

Step 1: Self-Assessment Scoring Directions

Aging is often more successful when it is accompanied by laughter. Whether this laughter occurs while reading, watching television, or interacting with others, it is of utmost importance to maintain a sense of humor.

The *Sense of Humor Self-Assessment* is designed to help you explore how well you are maintaining a sense of humor. On the previous page, add the numbers that you circled and write the score on the TOTAL line. You will receive a total in the range from 20 to 40. Then, transfer this number to the space below.

Sense of Humor TOTAL = _____

Profile Interpretation

Scores	Result	Indications
34 to 40	High	You are probably doing very well in maintaining your sense of humor.
27 to 33	Moderate	You are probably doing fairly well in maintaining your sense of humor.
20 to 26	Low	You are probably not doing well in maintaining your sense of humor.

Self-Assessment Descriptions

SENSE OF HUMOR – People scoring high on this scale are successfully maintaining a sense of humor. They are able to laugh at themselves, find humor in negative situations, and enjoy humor in the form of jokes, stories, books, and movies. Their sense of humor and ability to laugh easily reduces stress, helps cope with pain and creates empathy in social situations.

SUCCESSFUL AGING AND WELL-BEING

SENSE OF HUMOR

Step 2: Recognize and Develop a Support System

There are times when you may need help in seeing the humor in a difficult situation in order to relieve your stress. When this happens, a support system can help if you know people who are able to help you lighten up and find the humor in the situation. Complete the following table with people who might help you to do so.

Supporter	How This Person Can Support Me	How I Can Contact This Person
Example: My Partner	He can help me see the funny side of a situation without making the situation unimportant.	At home, call or text.

Keep this list handy. Call, email or text when you need support.

SUCCESSFUL AGING AND WELL-BEING

SENSE OF HUMOR

Step 3: Daily Living Journaling

It is important to explore the effectiveness of your sense of humor. The following sentence starters are designed to help you look at the humor in your life. Share your honest thoughts and emotions.

I am able to laugh at myself in the following situations: _____
_____
_____

I do not like laughing at myself in the following situations: _____
_____
_____

I will laugh at others in these situations: _____
_____
_____

I will not laugh at others in these situations: _____
_____
_____

I believe that a sense of humor can help me in these situations: _____
_____
_____

My sense of humor allows me to _____
_____
_____
_____
_____

SENSE OF HUMOR

Step 4: Set Goals

Successful aging calls for people to be able to find humor in a variety of situations and circumstances. For your action plan, identify aspects of your sense of humor you want to change, set specific goals to achieve this change, and notice how your life will be less stressful.

Goals need to be SMART:

Specific, **M**easureable, **A**ttainable, **R**ealistic, and **T**ime-Specific

Goals	How I Will Measure This Goal	How This Goal is Attainable and Realistic	Time Deadline	How This Will Help Me
Example: I will remember that people are laughing with me, not at me.	I will note the times I am not offended and realize they are teasing.	I will be aware and that will help me to be less sensitive when teased.	One month from now.	I will build better relationships with others.

If you are having trouble identifying goals, consult TIPS, page 91.

SUCCESSFUL AGING AND WELL-BEING

SENSE OF HUMOR

Step 5: Monitor My Humor Behavior

People who exhibit a sense of humor are able to find laughter in negative situations and maintain a positive outlook in life. In the table that follows, set some goals for enhancing your sense of humor. Periodic re-evaluation of your goals will help you to do so. Once you reach a goal, set new ones to improve or maintain your sense of humor even more. Use a separate page for each change.

EXAMPLE:

My humor behavior change   To spend time with playful people.

My goal   To laugh more in my daily life.

Date	My Accomplishment	How It Felt
June 12	I have found that when others laugh, it's easy for me to laugh.	It felt great!

✂ -

Humor

My humor behavior change _____

My goal _____

Date	My Accomplishment	How It Felt

SUCCESSFUL AGING AND WELL-BEING

SENSE OF HUMOR

Step 5: Monitor My Laughter Behavior

In the spaces that follow, identify what makes you laugh the most. Below, write how you are able to find humor in a variety of ways and how this humor benefits you.

Makes Me Laugh	Name the Most Humorous in Each Category	How This Humor Affects Me
Movies		
Television Shows		
Books		
People		
Situations		
Activities		
Stories		
Other		

SUCCESSFUL AGING AND WELL-BEING

SENSE OF HUMOR

Step 5: Monitor My Sense of Humor Quotation Behavior

In the spaces that follow, react to the quotation below.

> *A sense of humor... is needed armor. Joy in one's heart and some laughter on one's lips is a sign that the person down deep has a pretty good grasp of life.*
>
> ~ Hugh Sidey

How does your sense of humor provide armor for you?

_____
_____
_____
_____

What is the joy in your heart?

_____
_____
_____
_____

At what do you enjoy laughing?

_____
_____
_____
_____

How does your sense of humor provide you with a good grasp of life?

_____
_____
_____
_____

SUCCESSFUL AGING AND WELL-BEING

SENSE OF HUMOR

Step 6: Reward Myself

A positive sense of humor is essential as you age.
To age successfully you need to identify ways to laugh more often.

To do so, reward yourself with the ability to laugh.

In turn, you will be rewarded with the following bonuses in your life:

☺ Laughter increases hope.
☺ Laughter gives you energy.
☺ Laughter decreases anxiety.
☺ Laughter increases optimism.
☺ Laughter reduces depression.
☺ Laughter increases resilience.
☺ Laughter increases friendliness.
☺ Laughter increases self-esteem.
☺ Laughter connects us with others.
☺ Laughter helps you cope with pain.
☺ Laughter decreases blood pressure.
☺ Laughter inspires closer relationships.
☺ Laughter produces a feeling of relaxation.
☺ Laughter creates empathy in a social situation.
☺ Laughter produces a general sense of well-being.
☺ Laughter makes others laugh, even if it's not very funny.
☺ Laughter distracts. When you laugh you stop being angry.
☺ Laughter elevates your mood and moods of those around you.
☺ Laughter releases endorphins, which are the body's natural painkillers.
☺ Laughter reduces stress levels. It is an excellent stress management technique.
☺ Laughter is contagious. One person laughs and soon everyone in the room is laughing.

SUCCESSFUL AGING AND WELL-BEING

SENSE OF HUMOR

Step 7: Tips For Motivated Behavior Modifications

Opportunities to incorporate laughter into your everyday life:

- A smile is the beginning of laughter. Like laughter, it's contagious. When you look at someone or see something even mildly pleasing, practice smiling.

- Ask yourself, "What's the funniest thing that happened to me today? This week? In my life?"

- Check out your bookstore's humor section.

- Consider the good things in your life. This will distance you from negative thoughts that are a barrier to humor and laughter.

- Cuddle a pet.

- Do something silly.

- Enjoy a laughter yoga class.

- Go to a live comedy club.

- Host game night with friends.

- Keep a laughter journal. Write down all of the humorous things that happen to you daily. If you want, share your journal with others.

- Make time for fun activities (e.g. bowling, miniature golfing, karaoke).

- Play with children.

- Read the comics and cartoons in the newspaper.

- Seek out people who laugh easily and appropriately.

- Share a funny story.

- Spend time with fun, playful people. These are people who laugh easily, both at themselves and at life's absurdities, and who routinely find the humor in everyday events.

- Watch a funny movie or television show.

- When you hear laughter, move toward it.

SECTION VI
SOCIAL CONNECTIONS

Aging presents an opportunity to rethink our social and personal lives in order to ensure the dignity and welfare of each individual.

— **Daisaku Ikeda**

Name_____

Date_____

SUCCESSFUL AGING AND WELL-BEING

SOCIAL CONNECTIONS

Section I: Skills Emphasized in Each Activity Handout

Step 1: Self-Assessment
Respond to a set of prompts, self-score, and interpret personal profile on three scales: humanitarianism, active life, and social network.

Step 2: Recognize and Develop a Support System
Identify possible social connections supporters, types of support they can provide, and their contact information.

Step 3: Relationships Journaling
Describe situations in which help is needed. Identify three supporters, explain how the support can be mutual, and ways to show appreciation.

Step 4: Set Goals
Set goals that are specific, measureable, attainable, realistic, and time-specific. Identify ways to improve and maintain social connections. Note how these goals enhance successful aging.

Step 5: Monitor My Humanitarian Behavior
Identify a behavioral change and goal related to humanitarianism. Document dates, accomplishments, and resultant feelings on a behavioral log.

Monitor My Humanitarian Relationship Behavior
Name ways to help specific people. Share what helping others would mean to oneself.

Monitor My Active Life Behavior
Identify a behavioral change and goal related to an active life. Document dates, accomplishments, and resultant feelings on a behavioral log.

Monitor My Activities Behavior
Identify current activities from an extensive list of clubs/groups. Select additional activities one might join. Acknowledge the possibility of starting a new club/group.

Monitor Developing My Social Network Behavior
Identify a behavioral change and goal related to one's social network. Document dates, accomplishments, and resultant feelings on a behavioral log.

Monitor My Social Network Behavior
Name people to get to know better, reasons for establishing the social connections, and ways to include new social connections into one's social network. Note possible difficulties and ways to begin establishing a social network.

Step 6: Reward Myself
Reward self by selecting from an extensive list of small rewards. Personalize a quote by naming a person to forgive and to be reunited with.

Step 7: Tips for Motivated Behavior Modification
Acknowledge suggestions in these social connection categories: humanitarian, active lifestyle, and social network.

SUCCESSFUL AGING AND WELL-BEING

SOCIAL CONNECTIONS

Step 1: Self-Assessment Introduction and Directions

As time goes on, it can be difficult to maintain quality relationships. People have losses: partners, family, and friends pass away, move away, have different social needs and/or lose interest in the same activities. However, it is important to be willing to develop and maintain new and compatible relationships.

The *Social Connections Self-assessment* is designed to help you become aware of the quality relationships in your life.

This self-assessment contains 24 statements. Read each of the statements and decide how the statement applies to you. If it's true, circle the number 3. If it's somewhat true, circle the number 2. If it's not true, circle the number 1.

In the following example, circled number 2 indicates the statement is somewhat true for the person completing the self-assessment.

Answer all of the questions to the best of your ability using the following scale:

TRUE   SOMEWHAT TRUE   NOT TRUE

	TRUE	**SOMEWHAT TRUE**	**NOT TRUE**
I am concerned about the welfare of others.	3	(2)	1

This is not a test and there are no right or wrong answers. Do not spend too much time thinking about your answers. Your initial response will be the most true for you. Be sure to respond to every statement.

SUCCESSFUL AGING AND WELL-BEING

SOCIAL CONNECTIONS

Step 1: Self-Assessment

	TRUE	SOMEWHAT TRUE	NOT TRUE
I am concerned about the welfare of others	3	2	1
I enjoy helping people less fortunate than me	3	2	1
I like to hear others' stories	3	2	1
I genuinely care about other people	3	2	1
I like to help others without gain for myself	3	2	1
I do things for others	3	2	1
I have empathy for people	3	2	1
I feel fulfilled and energized when helping others	3	2	1

H TOTAL = _____

	TRUE	SOMEWHAT TRUE	NOT TRUE
I like playing cards or games	3	2	1
I enjoy visiting with people in-person	3	2	1
I like go out to eat with other people	3	2	1
I go to the movies with others	3	2	1
I watch TV and/or discuss the TV shows with others	3	2	1
I belong to a group, club, and/or house of worship	3	2	1
I enjoy the outdoors and nature with others	3	2	1
I exercise with others	3	2	1

A TOTAL = _____

	TRUE	SOMEWHAT TRUE	NOT TRUE
I have many friends and social contacts	3	2	1
I see and talk to people each week	3	2	1
I have contact with people whose interests are similar to mine	3	2	1
I enjoy the friends I have	3	2	1
I have a virtual network (media sites, email, blogs, etc.)	3	2	1
I know my neighbors and spend time with them	3	2	1
I know people I can count on	3	2	1
I have a network of family and friends to help in times of need	3	2	1

S TOTAL = _____

SUCCESSFUL AGING AND WELL-BEING

SOCIAL CONNECTIONS

Step 1: Self-Assessment Scoring Directions

The self-assessment you completed will help you explore your current social connections. Add the numbers you circled for each section and write that score on the line marked TOTAL at the end of the section. Then transfer those totals to the spaces below and add your three scores to get your Grand Total:

H. Humanitarianism   Total = _____
A. Active Life   Total = _____
S. Social Network   Total = _____
                                Grand TOTAL = _____

Profile Interpretation

Individual Scores	Grand Total	Result	Indications
19 to 24	57 to 72	High	If you score in the high range, you tend to be functioning well with your social connections.
14 to 18	40 to 56	Moderate	If you score in the moderate range, you tend to be functioning fairly well with your social connections.
8 to 13	24 to 39	Low	If you score in the low range, you are not functioning very well with your social connections.

Self-Assessment Descriptions

HUMANITARIANISM – People scoring high on this self-assessment tend to be concerned for the welfare of other people. They are empathic and supportive, and tend to enjoy helping others for the sake of helping, not for any reward in return.

ACTIVE LIFE – People scoring high on this self-assessment tend to have enjoyable active relationships with others.

SOCIAL NETWORK – People scoring high on this self-assessment tend to have a network of family and friends whom they can count on for companionship and support.

GRAND TOTAL – People scoring high on the grand total are humanitarians, care about others; live an active life with other people; and have an involved social network.

SUCCESSFUL AGING AND WELL-BEING

SOCIAL CONNECTIONS

Step 2: Recognize and Develop a Support System

Your approach to daily life has a profound effect on your social interactions. Identify the people in your life who will support you and ask them if they would be willing to help you in your efforts to grow in this area.

Supporter	How This Person Can Support Me	How I Can Contact This Person
Example: Dale, my next door neighbor.	*He knows everyone in the neighborhood and can introduce me to more people.*	*Phone: 000-000-0000.*

Keep this list handy. Call, email or text when you need support.

SUCCESSFUL AGING AND WELL-BEING

SOCIAL CONNECTIONS

Step 3: Daily Living Journaling

With relationships, caring about and supporting each other is important, especially as we get older. It will be helpful to explore some of those caring and supportive relationships.

In what types of stressful situations do you ask for, or need, support?

_____

_____

_____

Who are three people (family, friend, medical personnel) who are supportive of you?

1 _____

2 _____

3 _____

How do these three people support you?

1 _____

2 _____

3 _____

How do you support these three people?

1 _____

2 _____

3 _____

How do you show these three people that you appreciate and care about them?

1 _____

2 _____

3 _____

SUCCESSFUL AGING AND WELL-BEING

SOCIAL CONNECTIONS

Step 4: Set Goals

It is imperative to have goals to develop and/or maintain your caring and humanitarianism, lead an active life, and have a social network. Well-conceived action plans help you stay motivated as you work toward your goals. Complete the action plan below, noting the SMART steps required to reach your ultimate goals.

Goals need to be SMART:

Specific, **M**easureable, **A**ttainable, **R**ealistic, and **T**ime-Specific

Goals	How I Will Measure This Goal	How This Goal is Attainable and Realistic	Time Deadline	How This Will Help Me
Example: To meet more people.	By the number of new people I meet.	Yes. I will be more assertive. I have been sitting back and waiting for people to come to me.	End of the month.	I will have more people in my life.

If you are having trouble identifying goals, consult TIPS, page 108.

SUCCESSFUL AGING AND WELL-BEING

SOCIAL CONNECTIONS

Step 5: Monitor My Humanitarian Behavior

Social intelligence involves meeting new people, having effective social relationships and enjoying close relationships. Humanitarian people help others without the need for compensation. The table below will help you to keep track of your progress. Keeping track of caring about others will help you know when you are making positive changes in your behavior. Periodically re-evaluate your successes and setbacks. Once you reach your goal(s), set new ones to improve or maintain what you have already achieved. Use a separate page for each change.

EXAMPLE:

My humanitarian behavior change To spend time with playful people.

My goal To laugh more in my daily life.

Date	My Accomplishment	How It Felt
Sept. 12	I spoke with my neighbor and instead of complaining, I listened to her story.	It felt good to help her by listening. It also helped me to realize that I'm not the only person with concerns.

✂ -

Humanitarian

My humanitarian behavior change _____

My goal _____

Date	My Accomplishment	How It Felt

SUCCESSFUL AGING AND WELL-BEING

SOCIAL CONNECTIONS

Step 5: Monitor Humanitarian Relationship Behavior

Complete the table below to help you identify people you can add to your relationship network.

People to Add to My Relationship Network	How this Relationship Could Help Them	What Would this Mean to Me
Example: My sister-in-law	She's been very lonely since my brother passed away.	We could share stories about him and family. I'd like that and I know she would too.

SOCIAL CONNECTIONS

Step 5: Monitor My Active Life Behavior

Successful aging is largely determined by individual lifestyle choices. Enjoying an active lifestyle is extremely important. Through the table below, you will monitor your progress toward being as active as you can possibly be. Re-evaluate your goals as you develop more confidence in this process. Once you reach your goal(s), set new ones to improve or maintain what you have already achieved. Use a separate page for each change.

EXAMPLE:

My active life behavior change <u>I need to get out more.</u>

My goal <u>Every day do some activity away from home.</u>

Date	My Accomplishment	How It Felt
Nov. 22	I joined a book club.	I'm excited!

Active Life

My active life behavior change _____

My goal _____

Date	My Accomplishment	How It Felt

SUCCESSFUL AGING AND WELL-BEING

SOCIAL CONNECTIONS

Step 5: Monitor My Activities Behavior

There are many ways of staying active! Complete the table below by checking off your status for each type of club or group.

Clubs or Groups	I Do it Already	I Wouldn't Consider It	I Will Look Into It	I'm In!
Art				
Astronomy				
Bible Study				
Bike				
Birding				
Book				
Cards				
Ceramics/Clay				
Computer				
Concert				
Crafts				
Dance				
Day Trip				
Dinner				
Drumming				
Exercise				
Flower Arranging				
Games				
Genealogy				
Golf, Tennis, Bocce, Bowl				
Government Affairs				
Knit, Quilt, Crochet, Sew				
Learning				
Models				
Museum				
Neighborhood				
Scupture				
Singing				
Singles				
Swim				
Water Exercise				
Woodworking				
Writing				
Zumba				
Other				
Other				
Other				
Other				
Other				

If you can't find a local club, start one!

SUCCESSFUL AGING AND WELL-BEING

SOCIAL CONNECTIONS

Step 5: Monitor Developing My Social Network Behavior

People who age successfully have a network of family and friends with whom to share their lives. Monitoring your progress toward your goals of enhancing the number and quality of your relationships will help you tremendously. Periodic re-evaluations promote your success. Once you reach your goal(s), set new ones to improve or maintain what you have already achieved. Use a separate page for each change.

EXAMPLE:

My social network behavior change I want to have a closer relationship with my family.

My goal To reach out to my adult children more often without complaining and listening to them.

Date	My Accomplishment	How It Felt
May 5	I phoned my son and talked for two hours.	I felt relieved he was happy to hear from me.

Social Network

My social network behavior change _____

My goal _____

Date	My Accomplishment	How It Felt

SUCCESSFUL AGING AND WELL-BEING

SOCIAL CONNECTIONS

Step 5: Monitor My Social Network Behavior

Complete the following table to explore how you could build your social network.

Someone I Would Like to Get to Know Better	Why?	How I Can Get to Know this Person

What is difficult about developing your social network?

_____
_____
_____
_____

Describe what it will take to get you started.

_____
_____
_____
_____

SOCIAL CONNECTIONS

Step 6: Reward Myself

People who age successfully are interested in developing relationships with others. However, by giving yourself small rewards, you will maintain your motivation. This will motivate you to duplicate this behavior more. The challenge is to decide what reward would motivate you to reach your goal. Your reward needs to be something that will give you the incentive to achieve your goals. It needs to be within your budget and something you'll be excited about. If you are buying yourself something, be sure your reward is something you wouldn't ordinarily buy or do.

Some small possible rewards might include the following. Place a check mark in the boxes by those that might be possible small rewards for you:

- ☐ Ask for a new haircut.
- ☐ Buy a new outfit.
- ☐ Call someone you haven't talked with in years.
- ☐ Contact your favorite friend and make a date to go out on the town.
- ☐ Dance with no one around (or everyone).
- ☐ Enjoy a manicure and pedicure.
- ☐ Go out to eat at your favorite restaurant.
- ☐ Have something special to eat.
- ☐ If you live in a place with a lot of noise, find a place where you can enjoy quiet.
- ☐ Have one full day just for yourself to do whatever you want to do.
- ☐ Join a group.
- ☐ Make a date to go to a movie.
- ☐ Order in your favorite type of food.
- ☐ Plan a picnic
- ☐ Read a book that has been on your wish list.
- ☐ Rent a funny movie.
- ☐ Rescue a pet.
- ☐ Sign up for a class of interest.
- ☐ Take a dance lesson.
- ☐ Watch a movie that will give you a good laugh.
- ☐ Other_____
- ☐ Other_____

> *It takes one person to forgive, it takes two people to be reunited.*
>
> ~ Lewis B. Smedes

Whom would you like to forgive and then be reunited with?

_____

_____

_____

SUCCESSFUL AGING AND WELL-BEING

SOCIAL CONNECTIONS

Step 7: Tips For Motivated Behavior Modifications

Humanitarian

- Be as honest as you can when you are interacting with other people. Try to honor any obligations you make and attempt to be as reliable, dependable, and honest as you possibly can be.
- Help someone as often as possible, and expect nothing in return.
- Take responsibility for what you say – even in texts, social media forums, and e-mails. Self-disclosure can enhance your relationships by moving them to a new level of closeness and understanding.
- Be fully aware of your body language and the messages you are sending through your non-verbal communication.
- Do unto others as you would have them do unto you.

Active Life

Incorporate the following into your life.

- Adaptive exercise
- Aquatics
- Balance training
- Cardiovascular wellness
- Emotional wellness
- Environmental wellness
- Exercise
- Fall-risk management
- Intellectual wellness
- Mental wellness
- Motivation
- Nutrition
- Physical wellness
- Social wellness
- Spiritual wellness
- Sports
- Strength training
- Weight management

Social Network

- Demonstrate empathy and truly care for other people and experience the world as they are experiencing it.
- Express your appreciation of other people by letting them know when they have helped you and tell them how you appreciate having them for friends.
- Be generous with praise and cautious with criticism.
- Take healthy social risks. Identify people whom you believe will enhance your life and take risks to develop friendships.
- Make relationships a priority in your life. Put time and effort into developing and maintaining healthy relationships with others.
- Be positive and upbeat in your interactions with others.
- If you feel a need to talk with a friend about your health, do so for five minutes, and then change the subject.

SECTION VII
PRODUCTIVE AGING

*No one can avoid aging,
but aging productively is something else.*

– **Katharine Graham**

Name_____

Date_____

SUCCESSFUL AGING AND WELL-BEING

PRODUCTIVE AGING

Section I: Skills Emphasized in Each Activity Handout

Step 1: Self-Assessment
Respond to a set of prompts, self-score, and interpret personal profile on three scales: education, work, volunteer, and fun activities.

Step 2: Recognize and Develop a Support System
Identify possible productivity supporters, types of support they can provide, and their contact information.

Step 3: Activities Journaling
Describe worries, medical situation, ability to care for self, and ways one finds meaning in life.

Step 4: Set Goals
Describe ways one engages in educational, work, volunteer and fun activities. Note how each activity contributes to productivity.

Step 5: Monitor My Worry Behavior
Identify a behavioral change and goal related to education. Document dates, accomplishments, and resultant feelings on a behavioral log.

Monitor My Education Behavior – Opportunities
Evaluate a list of educational opportunities by explaining why each is or is not appealing. Describe ways to begin preferred activities.

Monitor My Work Behavior
Identify a behavioral change and goal related to work. Document dates, accomplishments, and resultant feelings on a behavioral log.

Monitor My Work Behavior – Opportunities
Evaluate a list of work opportunities by explaining why each is or is not appealing. Describe ways to begin preferred activities.

Monitor My Volunteer Behavior
Identify a behavioral change and goal related to volunteering. Document dates, accomplishments, and resultant feelings on a behavioral log.

Monitor My Volunteer Behavior – Opportunities
Evaluate a list of volunteer opportunities by explaining why each is or is not appealing. Describe ways to begin preferred activities.

Monitor My Fun Behavior
Identify a behavioral change and goal related to fun. Document dates, accomplishments, and resultant feelings on a behavioral log.

Monitor My Fun Behavior – Activities
Evaluate a list of fun activities by explaining why each is or is not appealing. Describe ways to begin preferred activities.

Step 6: Reward Myself
Identify rewards that are exciting, meaningful, small, large, free, affordable, can be enjoyed alone, and can be enjoyed with others.

Step 7: Tips for Motivated Behavior Modification
Acknowledge suggestions in these productivity categories: education, work, volunteer, and fun.

SUCCESSFUL AGING AND WELL-BEING

PRODUCTIVE AGING

Step 1: Self-Assessment Introduction and Directions

In order to age successfully, many people feel it is important to use their time well and productively. When using time productively, life remains full of hope and satisfaction. Productive people feel useful and have a positive attitude.

This self-assessment will help you identify how effectively you are using your time.

Circle the YES or NO answer that describes you. If the item does not apply to you, circle N/A (Not Applicable to me). In the following example, the circled NO indicates that the statement is not descriptive of the person completing the inventory.

My Educational Activities ...
  Help me interact with others . . . . YES   (NO)   N/A

This is not a test and there are no right or wrong answers. Do not spend too much time thinking about your answers. Your initial response will be the most true for you. Be sure to respond to every statement.

SUCCESSFUL AGING AND WELL-BEING

PRODUCTIVE AGING

Step 1: Self-Assessment

My Educational Activities ...

Help me interact with others	YES	NO	N/A
Help me to be a good conversationalist	YES	NO	N/A
Help me pass the time	YES	NO	N/A
Help my personal development	YES	NO	N/A
Help my brain to stay sharp	YES	NO	N/A
Help me to keep learning something new	YES	NO	N/A
Help me learn something I have always been interested in	YES	NO	N/A
Help me stay up to date	YES	NO	N/A

E. TOTAL = _____

My Working Activities ...

Help me interact with other people	YES	NO	N/A
Help me role-model my "old-fashioned" ethics	YES	NO	N/A
Help me pass the time	YES	NO	N/A
Help me feel productive	YES	NO	N/A
Help my brain stay sharp	YES	NO	N/A
Help keep me independent	YES	NO	N/A
Help me feel good by continuing to use my skills	YES	NO	N/A
Help me pay for something I couldn't otherwise afford	YES	NO	N/A

W. TOTAL = _____

My Volunteer Activities ...

Help me interact with other people	YES	NO	N/A
Help me make the world a better place	YES	NO	N/A
Help me pass the time	YES	NO	N/A
Help me share my experience	YES	NO	N/A
Help my brain stay sharp	YES	NO	N/A
Help keep my mind off myself	YES	NO	N/A
Help me feel good by helping others	YES	NO	N/A
Help me give back for all the help I have received	YES	NO	N/A

V. TOTAL = _____

My Fun Activities ...

Help me interact with other people	YES	NO	N/A
Help me feel younger	YES	NO	N/A
Help me pass the time	YES	NO	N/A
Help me feel good about myself	YES	NO	N/A
Help me have a great time and forget my problems	YES	NO	N/A
Help me have something to look forward to	YES	NO	N/A
Help me want to get dressed and ready to go	YES	NO	N/A
Help me recognize which friends I have fun with	YES	NO	N/A

F. TOTAL = _____

PRODUCTIVE AGING

Step 1: Self-Assessment Scoring Directions

The *Productive Aging Self-Assessment* is designed to measure how much satisfaction you are receiving from your educational, work, volunteer, and fun activities. For each of the sections on the self-assessment you completed, count the YES responses you circled for each of the four sections. Place that total on the line marked TOTAL at the end of each section.

- E. My Educational Activities   Total = _____
- W. My Work Activities   Total = _____
- V. My Volunteer Activities   Total = _____
- F. My Fun Activities   Total = _____

Profile Interpretation

Scores	Result	Indications
6 to 8	High	You are spending your time productively. Continue your education, work, volunteer, and/or fun activities.
3 to 5	Moderate	You are spending your time somewhat productively. Consider finding more education, work, volunteer, and/or fun activities.
0 to 2	Low	You are not spending your time productively. Consider engaging in education, work, volunteering, and/or fun activities.

Self-Assessment Descriptions

MY EDUCATIONAL ACTIVITIES – People scoring high on this self-assessment tend to engage in activities that keep them always learning something new.

MY WORK ACTIVITIES – People scoring high on this self-assessment tend to continue to work and are productive.

MY VOLUNTEER ACTIVITIES – People scoring high on this self-assessment tend to participate in volunteer activities, helping others and being productive.

MY FUN ACTIVITIES – People scoring high on this self-assessment tend to engage in fun activities, usually helping others to have fun also. They lead an enjoyable, productive life.

SUCCESSFUL AGING AND WELL-BEING

PRODUCTIVE AGING

Step 2: Recognize and Develop a Support System

It is important to examine how your current support system is helping you achieve your productivity goals. Not every supportive person in your life will fit this bill; so now is the time to identify those who can support you in your efforts to grow, and how they can help you. Different people can be supportive in different ways. Complete the following table with people who currently, and with people who might, support you with your education, work, volunteer, and fun activities.

Supporter	How This Person Can Support Me	How I Can Contact This Person
Example: My friend Sammie	She can help me to identify fun activities I am able to do.	phone or text 000-135-7913 email Friend@xyz.com .

Keep this list handy. Call, email or text when you need support.

SUCCESSFUL AGING AND WELL-BEING

PRODUCTIVE AGING

Step 3: Activities Journaling

Aging successfully means continuing to engage in satisfying educational, work, volunteer, and fun activities. The following journaling questions are designed to help you think carefully about how productive you currently are. Answer them honestly to highlight your insight into your current level of successful aging.

In what ways are you engaged in educational activities?

_____

_____

How do these educational activities help you to be productive?

_____

_____

In what ways are you engaged in work activities?

_____

_____

How do these work activities help you to be productive?

_____

_____

In what ways are you engaging in volunteer activities?

_____

_____

How do these volunteer activities help you to be productive?

_____

_____

In what ways are you engaging in fun activities?

_____

_____

How do these fun activities help you to be productive?

_____

_____

SUCCESSFUL AGING AND WELL-BEING

PRODUCTIVE AGING

Step 4: Set Goals

It is important to set goals for effectively using your time in a productive way! The next step is to set specific goals to provide yourself with educational, work, volunteer, and/or fun activities. The action plan that follows will help you to achieve your goals by keeping you motivated. Complete the action plan below, noting the SMART steps required to reach your goals.

Goals need to be SMART:

Specific, **M**easureable, **A**ttainable, **R**ealistic, and **T**ime-Specific

Goals	How I Will Measure This Goal	How This Goal is Attainable and Realistic	Time Deadline	How This Will Help Me
Example: I want to volunteer part-time at the veterinarian's office.	By how much I enjoy it.	Yes, I can make sure I get up early in the morning. I love animals and people!	Immediately.	I will feel needed.

If you are having trouble identifying goals, consult TIPS, page 126.

PRODUCTIVE AGING

Step 5: Monitor My Education Behavior

People who age successfully continue to engage in satisfying educational activities. Monitor your progress toward your goals by keeping track of your behaviors below. Periodic re-evaluations support your success. Once you reach your goal(s), set new ones to improve or maintain what you have already achieved. Use a separate page for each change.

EXAMPLE:

My education behavior change   <u>I want to audit some college courses.</u>

My goal   <u>To complete a degree.</u>

Date	My Accomplishment	How It Felt
Dec. 5	I enrolled in an astronomy course at the local college.	I am very proud of myself.

Education

My education behavior change _____

My goal _____

Date	My Accomplishment	How It Felt

SUCCESSFUL AGING AND WELL-BEING

PRODUCTIVE AGING

Step 5: Monitor My Education Behavior - Opportunities

In the spaces that follow, identify some of the education opportunities that appeal to you, and note why or why not.

Education Opportunities	Why It Does or Does Not Appeal to Me	IF it Appeals to Me, How I Can Get Started
Online Courses		
Certification Program		
College Courses		
Workshops/Seminars		
Learning Institutes		
Intellectual Stimulation (Online brain games; written crosswords, Sudoku, word-finds, etc.)		
Other		
Other		
Other		

PRODUCTIVE AGING

Step 5: Monitor My Work Behavior

Many people who age successfully continue to engage in productive work opportunities. In the table that follows, monitor your progress in this area. Keeping track will help you follow your progress. Periodic re-evaluations are vital for your success. Once you reach your goal(s), set new ones to improve or maintain what you have already achieved. Use a separate page for each change.

EXAMPLE:

My work behavior change To begin working part-time.

My goal To make a little money and utilize my skills.

Date	My Accomplishment	How It Felt
March 3	I interviewed for a part-time accounting job during tax season.	Fulfilling.

Work

My work behavior change _____

My goal _____

Date	My Accomplishment	How It Felt

SUCCESSFUL AGING AND WELL-BEING

PRODUCTIVE AGING

Step 5: Monitor My Work Behavior - Opportunities

In the spaces that follow, identify some of the work opportunities that appeal to you and why.

Work Opportunities	Why It Does or Does Not Appeal to Me	If it Appeals to Me, How I Can Get Started
Work Part-time		
Work as a Consultant		
Start My Own Business		
Speak at Conferences		
Teach		
Other		
Other		
Other		

SUCCESSFUL AGING AND WELL-BEING

PRODUCTIVE AGING

Step 5: Monitor My Volunteer Behavior

Many people who age successfully continue to engage in productive volunteer activities. In the table that follows, monitor your progress in this area. Keeping track will help you follow your progress. Periodic re-evaluations are vital for your success. Once you reach your goal(s), set new ones to improve or maintain what you have already achieved. Use a separate page for each change.

EXAMPLE:

My volunteer behavior change   To volunteer at a school as a teacher's helper.

My goal   To help kids and help the teacher also.

Date	My Accomplishment	How It Felt
Jan. 30	I am helping kids in first grade with their reading.	SO fulfilling. I love children and my grandchildren live far away.

Volunteer

My volunteer behavior change _____

My goal _____

Date	My Accomplishment	How It Felt

SUCCESSFUL AGING AND WELL-BEING

PRODUCTIVE AGING

Step 5: Monitor My Volunteer Behavior - Opportunities

Volunteering is rewarding. It makes you feel like you are accomplishing something, that you are giving back and that you are helping people. Volunteering also gives you the opportunity to meet people, make new friends, and get out of your living space. You can volunteer a day or two a week, or in some cases, even a few hours a day.

Volunteer Opportunities	Why It Does or Does Not Appeal to Me	If it Appeals to Me, How I Can Get Started
Teach classes at retirement places		
Run errands for people in need		
Mentor and/or consult		
Visit people who are ill		
Read to children in a hospital		
Other		
Other		
Other		

SUCCESSFUL AGING AND WELL-BEING

PRODUCTIVE AGING

Step 5: Monitor My Fun Behavior

People who age successfully continue to engage in productive fun, play, and leisure activities. Use the table below to set goals, keep track of your behaviors, and monitor your progress. Once you reach your goal(s), set new ones to improve or maintain what you have already achieved. Use a separate page for each change.

EXAMPLE:

My fun behavior change <u>I started going to ballroom dances.</u>

My goal <u>To still enjoy my favorite activities from the past.</u>

Date	My Accomplishment	How It Felt
Feb. 4	I went to my first dance and met nice people.	I felt proud of myself.

✂ --

Fun

My fun behavior change _____

My goal _____

Date	My Accomplishment	How It Felt

SUCCESSFUL AGING AND WELL-BEING

PRODUCTIVE AGING

Step 5: Monitor My Fun Behavior – Activities

Active seniors know how to have a fun time with activities for the body, mind, and spirit. A full, vibrant, and productive life benefits from fun activities. There are many fun activities people can take part in to keep their bodies exercised, minds sharp, and spirits up. Spending time outdoors, playing indoor games, or doing things they love can benefit their overall well-being.

Fun Opportunities	Why It Does or Does Not Appeal to Me	If it Appeals to Me, How I Can Get Started
Games - Puzzles		
Dancing - Singing		
Concerts - Plays		
Funny Movies or TV		
Picnic - Fishing		
Sports: Watch or Play		
Other		
Other		
Other		
Other		

SUCCESSFUL AGING AND WELL-BEING

PRODUCTIVE AGING

Step 6: Reward Myself

Identifying ways to use your time productively is important! To stay motivated, you need to give yourself rewards. Your reward needs to be something that will give you the incentive to achieve your goals. It needs to be within your budget and something you'll be excited about. If you are buying yourself something, be sure your reward is something you wouldn't ordinarily buy or do.

Brainstorm possible rewards, but remember that …
- **Rewards should be meaningful to you**
- **Rewards can be big … or they can be small**
- **Rewards do not have to cost money to be fun**
- **Rewards should be affordable**
- **Rewards can be enjoyed alone or with people who support you**

You deserve a pat on the back for the good work you are completing in this section. Rewards help you to pay attention to your triumphs, not your setbacks. Rewards will create good feelings and propel you to want to work harder on reaching your goals. In the blocks that follow, draw or doodle four rewards you will give yourself when you have achieved four new goals.

SUCCESSFUL AGING AND WELL-BEING

PRODUCTIVE AGING

Step 7: Tips For Motivated Behavior Modifications

Education Activities:

- Talk with your local college admissions office about taking classes.
- Look around your community for various learning opportunities. Your local library, community college, and retirement community often offer classes, courses, workshops, and seminars on a variety of topics.
- Consider projects such as tracing your genealogy
- Learn more about how to use different types of technology or photography,
- Play a musical instrument, learn a second language or join a book club.
- Take an online course at the local college or community college.
- Check out religious or spiritual classes or retreats.

Work Activities:

- Meet with a SCORE representative to talk about starting a small business.
- Seek part-time jobs that may be of interest to you.
- Use your work skills and become a handy-person.
- Pet sit for people going on vacation.
- House watch for people who go on vacations.
- Become a seamstress from your home.
- Tutor math or a language.

Volunteer Activities:

- Volunteer to help a cause of interest to you.
- Using your skills and interests, share these to benefit other people.
- Read to children in schools.
- Baby sit.
- Visit children in the hospital.
- Train you dog to be a service dog and take him/her to visit hospital patients.
- Bring food to a neighbor who can't get out.

Fun Activities:

- Engage in social activities with friends.
- Enjoy concerts, museums, zoos, theater, movies, etc.
- Look for opportunities to spend time with people whose interests are similar to yours.
- Host parties or get-togethers at your house to socialize and meet new people.
- Join clubs that cater to people with the same interests as yours.
- Go to ballgames, or play ball with others.
- Invite friends over to watch a movie, tennis match, ball game, etc.

Whole Person Associates is the leading publisher of training resources for professionals who empower people to create and maintain healthy lifestyles. Our creative resources will help you work effectively with your clients in the areas of stress management, wellness promotion, mental health, and life skills.

Please visit us at our web site: **WholePerson.com**. You can check out our entire line of products, place an order, request our print catalog, and sign up for our monthly special notifications.

Whole Person Associates

800-247-6789
Books@WholePerson.com